X

Thinking skills
A teacher's guide

Mike Jeffries and
Trevor Hancock

Introduction

Lesson plans

> *'Thought is a bird of space,*
> *that, in a cage of words,*
> *may indeed unfold its wings*
> *but cannot fly'*
>
> Kalil Gibran; 'The Prophet'
>
> Surely our task as teachers is to not only enable children to operate within the 'cage of words' but also help them 'fly' as thinkers and learners.

Published by Hopscotch Educational Publishing Ltd,
29 Waterloo Place, Leamington Spa CV32 5LA
(Tel: 01926 744227)

© 2002 Hopscotch Educational Publishing

Written by Mike Jeffries and Trevor Hancock
Series design by Blade Communications
Illustrated by Martha Hardy
Cover illustrated by Pat Murray
Printed by Stephens and George Ltd

Mike Jeffries and Trevor Hancock hereby assert their moral right
to be identified as the authors of this work in accordance with the
Copyright, Designs and Patents Act, 1988.

ISBN 1-902239-92-X

Thinking about thinking

Learning is changing

Assumptions about learning – implicit in all things educational – have been challenged. This has occurred because the world is changing at a phenomenal rate; some reckon that scientific knowledge alone doubles every three and three-quarter years. Increasingly the economies of countries are being information-driven; the revolution in information and communication technology continues unabated and through the contribution of neuroscience we are able to make learning brain-compatible.

At a recent conference in Japan, 25 shifts in the development of learning were clearly identified. They included:

❑ A shift from the reception of knowledge to the creation of knowledge.

❑ A shift from the acquisition of knowledge to the management of knowledge.

❑ A shift from thought systems to the use of thinking tools.

The signs are now clearly evident that a revolution in learning is beginning to take place and at the centre of this revolution is the process of thinking.

As Professor David Perkins (Harvard University) suggested:

'Far from thinking coming after knowledge, knowledge comes on the coat-tails of thinking ... therefore, instead of knowledge-centred schools we need thinking-centred schools. This is no luxury, no Utopian vision of erudite and elitist education. These are the hard facts about the way that learning works.'

We have assumed for far too long that it is the school 'subjects' themselves that teach thinking. This fallacy is often supported by the intention that 'subjects' provide opportunities to promote thinking skills.

But when are children actually taught about thinking, how it works and how skills can be applied?

Around the world, initiatives in the direct teaching of thinking skills are flourishing. They range from Singapore's nationwide initiative, where momentum from the 'Thinking Schools – Learning Nation' movement is revolutionising the curriculum, to numerous research and development projects in the United States, Australia, Canada, New Zealand, Hong Kong and so on.

The UK response

Despite large-scale initiatives in educational development in Britain (National Curriculum, Literacy and Numeracy Strategies etc), little has been undertaken in the field of thinking skill development other than a few relatively small-scale projects. In the DfEE document 'Excellence in Schools' (1997) there was encouragement for more examples of the teaching of thinking skills to emerge, as research had previously shown there to be positive learning outcomes.

It has only been with the revision of the National Curriculum in 2000 that real opportunities have arisen for schools and teachers to tap into the potential to enhance learning through an increased focus on the direct development of children's thinking skills.

Alongside the introduction of the six 'Key Skills' (Communication, Application of number, ICT, Improving own learning and performance, Working with others and Problem solving) there is direct reference to five 'Thinking Skills':

❑ Information processing
❑ Reasoning
❑ Enquiry
❑ Creative thinking
❑ Evaluation

It is into this framework that this book is contextualised. It combines the requirements of all the National Curriculum Programmes of Study with those five thinking skills.

Making the thinking skills explicit gives us the opportunity to focus directly; to teach thinking. Thus the learners in our schools and classrooms are empowered to see the connections in learning, to understand how thinking and learning works and to apply the skills across and beyond the curriculum.

'Providing opportunities to promote thinking skills' does not ensure that children are taught the skills and can apply them across the curriculum. 'Awareness of' is not the same as 'doing'! I have an awareness that my car engine is repairable but I have no idea how to repair it. In developing ball-control skills in netball it is preferable to teach the skills specifically rather than just hope they will develop during a match.

In Holland children are not introduced to the game of football until they are aged eight; prior to that, ball skills are taught specifically. Only at eight are they given the opportunity to play a game in which the focus is application of the skills taught.

Children as thinkers

For more years than have been good for us in education we have played the 'Academic game' in our schools. Under the categorisation of subject headings, we have been manipulating information as knowledge in the hope that the children themselves will work out how the thoughts, ideas and underlying concepts are connected and 'how the information works'. But we have kept the rules of the 'Academic game' a mystery. The magic that is learning how to learn and think has been kept under wraps as though it was an unspoken prize accessible to the lucky (and clever) few.

How naive of us, then, to believe that our children have not worked all this out for themselves. Children know how learning works. They know how thinking happens.

They are asked to do both many, many times a day. It is just that in the 'Academic game' we have never found time to ask them or discuss with them ways of making learning and thinking more effective.

'Thinking is like a journey from one idea to the next,' said Alison, a nine-year-old in one Cognitive Classroom Project school.

She knows about thinking; she knows of its dynamic quality; she knows that it is about making connections

and is about movement between ideas and concepts. It is simply that no-one had ever asked her before!

'Thinking is like doing "join-the-dots"; you start on one thing, then you think, then you go to another thing,' replied Ashley, aged seven.

Even Ben, a philosophical and spiritual five-year-old, could describe the function and purpose of the mind.

'It's a place in your brain where you keep all your dreams. It's for memories and information as well.'

Ben has the basis upon which to build the structures that are metacognition; the ability to think about thinking.

The Cognitive Classroom

Outcomes from the Cognitive Classroom Project (1998 to present; a schools-based project to develop pupils' thinking skills) show, time after time, that not only do children have their own working knowledge of what thinking is, but also by involving themselves in the explicit articulation of its workings, they can often dramatically improve their thinking and learning potential.

Vanessa was one such child. Within a 30-minute introduction to a simple colour-referenced vocabulary for different thinking styles, she was not only able to display her working knowledge of the styles, but also could plan a sequence of foci for thinking that would help her explore a simple issue. For Vanessa, that thinking was power and it made a remarkable transformation in her self-esteem as a thinker and learner.

Consistently, outcomes from programmes and approaches to the teaching of thinking have shown a similar influence on self-esteem and confidence-building in thinking for learning and it should come as no surprise to us as teachers.

About this book

This book evolved as one of the many positive outcomes of The Cognitive Classroom Project (1998 to present). The Project is a practical response to the need for schools to consider ways of enhancing learning through the direct teaching of thinking skills. Discrete thinking skill programmes do exist and there are initiatives to introduce such skills into school subjects as discrete entities. However, no tools exist to empower teachers and learners to release the cross-curricular potential of the five National Curriculum thinking skills and to see their relevance within and beyond the school curriculum. This is the raison d'etre of this book.

Thinking skills is a practical, easy-to-use toolkit to support teachers. Practical thinking activities for Key Stage 1 and 2 children are provided and these can be used to introduce and develop specific thinking skills when appropriate to the needs of groups/classes of children or individual children.

Thinking skills enables you to plan explicit teaching of essential skills in support of learning activities across the curriculum. Children will also have the opportunity to make connections between the skills and real life situations, thus seeing the purpose and reason for learning.

For example, a teacher might be planning work in English that involves deduction from classifying skills. The chosen text may include actions taken by the main character and actions of others. A question may be asked as to who is to blame for a particular situation. If children have not been introduced to the skill of classifying information and do not have experience in applying that skill, then they will be unable to deduce from the text who is to blame.

This is explored in more detail in Chapter 3, 'Planning for thinking skills.

We have called the activities in this book 'THUNKS'. Each 'thunk' introduces and helps to teach a specific thinking skill.

'THUNKS' is an acronym for:

> THinking for
> UNderstanding and
> Knowledge in
> Subjects

Each 'thunk' is laid out on two pages and gives details and guidance for the teacher on the organisation and management of the activity plus a description of the activity and suggestions for extension activities. Some 'thunks' have a 'thinking frame' attached. This is a graphical organiser that children can use to organise their thinking.

Organising and managing the activity

Key skills – this refers to key skills that will be used during the 'thunk'.

Subject links – this refers to some of the subjects in which this skill could be further developed.

Aims – the particular aims of the 'thunk' relating specifically and solely to thinking skills.

Organisation – explains whether the 'thunk' is for individuals, pairs, groups or the whole class.

Time – this is an indication of the time each 'thunk' will take. This is for guidance only and teachers will need to use their professional judgement on the length of time needed to complete each section of the 'thunk'.

Resources – although we have endeavoured to keep the need for additional resources, other than paper for recording thinking and outcomes, to a minimum, there are occasions when the teacher will need to provide some. These are all readily available and most schools will already have them.

Outcomes – exactly what is expected to be achieved by the learners is detailed in this section.

The task – a description of the 'thunk' activity.

Assessment – what to assess and how to assess the children's thinking is described.

Teaching tip – this is where the teacher will find specific guidance on how to teach the 'thunk'. It is not a lesson plan but advice on the pace, structure and delivery of the activity. This is intended to be supportive without being too prescriptive and flexible enough to be relevant to all school situations.

Extension activities – a variety of ideas for developing the 'thunk' into other and often more challenging areas.

Thinking skills in the National Curriculum

In this chapter we shall be considering the National Curriculum with regard to the role of thinking skills. We shall examine and consider the following points.

- ❑ The aims, values and purposes of the National Curriculum.
- ❑ Key skills.
- ❑ Problem solving and the role of thinking skills within the problem-solving process.
- ❑ Thinking skills as identified within the National Curriculum.
- ❑ Embedding thinking skills within the National Curriculum.

There is clear evidence that Curriculum 2000 is in response to the acknowledgement that education needs to respond to a rapidly changing world and the opportunities and challenges this creates. There is a fundamental shift of emphasis towards the skills that individuals need, as well as the knowledge they should have and the concepts they should understand. Naturally specific subject skills are there, such as those required in numeracy, literacy, science and ICT; but in addition there are now some generic skills included. For instance, developing the skills of communication, improving own learning and performance and creative thinking. The rationale behind the new curriculum is explained in the opening section 'Aims, Values and Purposes' and is worth exploring in some detail if we are to begin to see how thinking skills fit into it.

Aims, values and purposes of Curriculum 2000

Following are a selection of key phrases from this opening section and our commentary on them. At this stage we have not provided detailed guidance on implementing these aims and values but raise some issues that you will need to address within your own school. (Words in italic are direct quotes from the document.)

The National Curriculum is an important element of the school curriculum.

Clearly it is not the sole curriculum that will be taught in your school. You will have your own school-initiated curriculum, which addresses the needs of your learners as identified by yourselves. This short statement gives schools a freedom that previously they may have perceived as being missing.

What is it in your school that you believe should be taught alongside, or as part of, the National Curriculum and how do you achieve this? Does it include thinking skills?

Foremost is a belief in education as a route to the spiritual, moral, social, cultural, physical and mental development and thus the well being of the individual.

This concerns the ability of individuals to make informed choices in their lives. If we teach children to think creatively, logically and laterally and to rationalise, assimilate and consider all the information and influences they experience, then they will be more able to make sound judgements.

AIM 1 : The school curriculum should aim to provide opportunities for all pupils to learn and to achieve.

- *The school curriculum should develop enjoyment of, and commitment to learning … and develop their confidence in their capacity to learn and work independently and collaboratively.*
- *… it should promote an enquiring mind and the capacity to think rationally… and prompt a personal response to a range of experiences and ideas.*
- *By providing rich and varied contexts for pupils the curriculum should enable them to think creatively and critically, to solve problems and to make a difference for the better.*
- *It should promote the opportunity to become creative, innovative, enterprising and capable of leadership to equip them for their future lives as workers and citizens.*

This aim emphasises that learning should be active rather than passive and that the curriculum should be more skills-based than knowledge-based. The curriculum should allow for awe and wonder and provide time for children to reflect on their learning, experiences and ideas. It should allow them to take risks and try things out for themselves, and to take responsibility for an idea or scheme and to run with it. There is a clear reference here to thinking. If children are to 'think rationally' and make a personal response to an experience they will need to have developed an awareness of self-evaluation and metacognition, ie the ability and disposition to 'think about their thinking'. There are huge implications here for the way in which we teach children and whether we give importance to the need for learners to be aware of the type of thinking they are using.

The issue of problem solving will be addressed later in this chapter.

> *AIM 2 : The school curriculum should aim to promote pupils' spiritual, moral, social and cultural development and prepare all pupils for the opportunities, responsibilities and experiences of life.*
>
> * *The school curriculum should pass on enduring values, develop pupils' integrity and autonomy …*
> * *It should equip pupils as consumers to make personal informed judgements and independent decisions and to understand their responsibilities and rights.*
> * *It should enable pupils to respond positively to opportunities, challenges, and responsibilities, to manage risk and to cope with change and adversity.*
> * *It should … equip them to make informed choices at school and throughout their lives …*

From this we can see that we need to provide children with challenges and the opportunity to take responsibility for their own thinking. We need to develop children's personal dispositions towards their learning, for example perseverance, self-evaluation, flexibility, an acceptance of what they cannot change and an ability to feel fulfilled. In short, enabling children to develop from dependent learners to becoming independent learners and thinkers.

The four main purposes of the National Curriculum

1 To establish an entitlement. *The National Curriculum secures for all pupils … an entitlement to a number of areas of learning and to develop knowledge, understanding, skills and attitudes necessary for their self-fulfilment and development as active and responsible citizens.*

For the first time one of those areas of learning includes thinking skills. It is our duty to ensure that our children have the capability to think in different ways appropriate to the situation they find themselves in, and are able to consider their own thinking and select the appropriate strategy or skill. By being able to do this they will become more 'self-fulfilled' and confident.

2 To establish standards. *The National Curriculum makes expectations of learning and attainment explicit to pupils, parents, teachers, governors, employers and the public, and establishes national standards for the performance of all pupils in the subjects it includes.*

There are tests on the 'core subjects' of English, mathematics and science but as yet we have no 'test' for assessing standards in children's thinking. Each school needs to consider how test results are used diagnostically to evaluate the quality of teaching and learning. It would be a mistake if we allowed ourselves to become too fixed upon these indicators. The best schools have identified and are using a much wider range of indicators, some of which may be focusing on children's learning, and in particular the way in which they learn. Now that thinking skills are included in the National Curriculum, schools must begin to address the issue of how they will assess these skills. We shall be considering this issue in detail in Chapter 2.

3 To promote continuity and coherence. *The National Curriculum contributes to a coherent national framework that promotes curriculum continuity and is sufficiently flexible to ensure progression in pupils' learning. … and provides a foundation for lifelong learning.*

Lifelong learning is a laudable idea but can only be achieved if pupils leave secondary school with the motivation and disposition to continue learning. It is essential that their perception of learning is that it is a self-fulfilling and rewarding activity, and that they recognise that learning is not restricted to the classroom. Confident and flexible thinkers are able to do this. Creating a culture and ethos that actively and explicitly promote this ideal within schools is a key element in enabling this to happen.

Is your school a 'cognitive' one? Is the development of thinking at the heart of what you do and the way in which you teach and expect children to learn?

4   To promote public understanding. *The National Curriculum increases public understanding of the work schools … It provides a common basis for discussion of educational issues among lay and professional groups, including pupils, parents, teachers, governors and employers.*

You read earlier about the global interest in thinking and that the dialogue concerning these issues is taking place in an increasing number of forums. One of the forums where it is happening least is within schools themselves. How often do we teachers talk explicitly about thinking with parents? We have already raised the need for establishing the right ethos and culture within schools, and it is essential that parents and all stakeholders within the school are aware of the place of thinking and cognition. Schools will need to 'educate' stakeholders about thinking skills and promote thinking at every opportunity.

How will your school go about achieving this paradigm shift in the understanding and attitude of stakeholders to the role of education?

Developing the school curriculum

While these four purposes (identified above) do not change over time, the curriculum itself cannot remain static. It must be responsive to changes in society and the economy, and changes in the nature of schooling itself. Teachers, individually and collectively, have to reappraise their teaching in response to the changing needs of their pupils and the impact of economic, social and cultural change. Education only flourishes if it successfully adapts to the demands and needs of the time.

The National Curriculum recognises the importance of thinking skills and the key skills required to be an effective and useful member of society. It has also begun to address the issue of how children learn across the curriculum, and that learning does not just happen in neat separate subject packages. Learning is far too complex and intricate for that. Thinking skills provide a set of common tools that facilitate learning in all subject areas.

'Improve the thinking to improve the learning.'

Key skills

The curriculum acknowledges that pupils *learn, practise, combine, develop and refine a wide range of skills across the National Curriculum* and that some of these skills are subject specific and some are common to several subjects. It also recognises that some skills are *universal and are embedded in the subjects of the National Curriculum and are essential to effective learning.*

There is, on page 20 of the *National Curriculum*, a crucial sentence that we believe begins to get to the heart of the matter about how children learn and think:

> *Pupils can be encouraged to reflect on what and on how they learn, and how these skills can be applied to different subjects, different problems and real life situations.*

The essential difference between that statement and what we are advocating is that we would not only 'encourage' children to reflect on their learning, but also actually teach the skills of reflection and self-evaluation.

In order for pupils to improve their learning and performance in education, work and life, the National Curriculum identifies six key skills.
* *Communication*
* *Application of number*
* *Information technology*
* *Working with others*
* *Improving own learning and performance*
* *Problem solving*

For the activities in this book we have identified how the thinking skills interrelate with these key skills and also some subject specific skills.

Communication

Communication includes speaking, listening, reading and writing. The ability to communicate effectively is an essential skill. To be effective the communicator has to take regard of the audience and the purpose of the communication and be flexible enough to respond to audience reaction. This will be improved when the communicator has well-developed thinking skills.

For example, take a familiar learning task for English – planning a story. Which thinking skill(s) should we expect the children to use? One of the key elements of creating a plot is to consider the consequences of an event or a character's actions or words. Clearly this involves some of the skills of enquiry – predicting outcomes, anticipating consequences.

Application of number

This includes mental calculation, use of mathematical language, calculations, data processing and problem solving. It is the ability to apply these skills and the ability to give reasons why they have been used that depends on thinking skills. Maths is a 'real life' skill and therefore generic thinking skills will often be used before specific maths skills are applied. Here metacognition (thinking about thinking) is at the fore. This is very true of data processing where children will be expected to analyse and interpret data and give reasons for their interpretations.

A group of Y5/6 children were asked to fill in a tally chart about how often they used a variety of forms of communication. These ranged from telephones to fax machines. After all the responses had been collected they had a more reliable database to start analysing and interpreting. The children were asked to make two statements based on their interpretations. The two most commonly expressed were:

a) The most common form of communication used was the television.
b) The least used form of communication used was the fax machine.

To arrive at these statements they had been using the mathematical skills of data handling. However, the next task presented to them was reliant on thinking skills. They were asked to say why they thought these two were the most and least commonly used. Among some of the responses were:

❑ 'Well nearly every, if not all, homes have got a TV so you would expect nearly all, if not all, children to have used one.'
❑ 'Children really like TV so you would expect them to use the TV a lot.'
❑ 'Not many homes have a fax machine because they are mostly used by businesses.'
❑ 'A lot of people use the computer to send e-mails instead because it's easier and more people have computers at home than have faxes.'

This was wonderful thinking by the children. They were no longer using maths skills but thinking skills instead. This led on to a fascinating discussion about how we would communicate in the future, and the limitations of some of the current forms of communication we use today. They were particularly excited by the thought of interactive television. 'Ask the audience' in 'Who Wants To Be A Millionaire?' takes on a whole new dimension!

Information technology

The key skill of information technology includes the ability to use a range of information sources and ICT tools to find, analyse, interpret, evaluate and present information for a range of purposes. *Skills include the ability to make critical and informed judgements about when and how to use ICT for maximum benefit in accessing information, in solving problems or for expressive work.* Under this section it states that the ability to use ICT information includes, amongst others, creative thinking skills. There are clear links here to a range of thinking skills that children will have to use in order to make these judgements. One set of thinking skills is to do with information processing and another critical thinking. In order to achieve some or all of the key skills, the learner will have to employ thinking skills first. ICT is perceived as being a separate subject in its own right and also a tool for learning right across the curriculum. We would argue that the same could be said of thinking skills.

Working with others

The key skill of working with others includes the ability to contribute to a range of group activities and discussions and to meet a challenge through cooperation with others. It is necessary for children to be able to consider different perspectives while working with others. In order to consider anything, one has to 'think' about the different aspects of the topic under consideration. We propose that the quality of the thinking will be improved if that thinking has some structure and the children have some tools to assist them. The activities in this book often refer to frames or structures and these are explored in more detail in the chapter about teaching approaches.

Improving own learning and performance

This involves children reflecting on and critically evaluating their work and what they have learned, and identifying ways to improve their own learning and performance. They need to be able to identify the purposes of learning, to reflect on the process of learning, to assess progress in learning, to identify obstacles or problems in learning and to plan ways to improve learning. This emphasises that the learner should be placed in the centre of the learning process, and that they should be actively involved in managing the process. One element of effective teaching is to share with the learner the purpose of the task or activity, to provide a clear statement of the learning objective. It is only by doing this that a child can reflect and judge whether they have met the objective and measure their progress towards achieving it. This is becoming common practice in schools and is an essential component in metacognition. A further implication of this key skill is that the learner needs to be able to recognise their own preferred learning style and be aware of a range of alternatives. In this way, ultimately they will be able to take responsibility for managing the learning process. This is truly active learning. It also means that until the child has reached complete independence they will need to be guided in this matter. Teachers need to give opportunities within the learning activities for children to develop and experiment with these different processes. **Matching the teaching to the desired learning process and objectives is therefore very important.** If children are expected to plan their own learning they will need to have a structure for thinking and the tools to think to enable effective planning.

Problem solving

This includes the skills of identifying and understanding a problem, planning ways to solve a problem, monitoring progress in tackling a problem and reviewing solutions to problems. There are several models for problem solving in common use but many are outdated and have been overtaken by recent research as discussed in the opening chapter. There is an assumption that just because we have a model of the process, children will be able to follow it and become problem solvers. This is a false assumption because it presupposes that the potential problem solver has the appropriate thinking skills and tools to successfully complete each stage of the model.

For example:
- being able to determine the immediate, medium- and long-term effects of an action or decision
- listing all the parts of a situation that should be considered
- targeting what needs to be thought about at any given moment
- foreseeing problems
- noting the information still needed in order to think about a situation
- prioritising

We must teach these skills if we want our children to develop the confidence to use any particular model your school promotes.

Thinking skills – learning to learn

There are five areas of thinking identified in the National Curriculum and the following thinking skills complement and support the key skills identified above.

Information-processing skills
- Locating and collecting information
- Sorting
- Classifying
- Sequencing
- Comparing and contrasting
- Analysing relationships

Reasoning skills

❑ Giving reasons for opinions and actions
❑ Drawing inferences
❑ Making deductions
❑ Explaining what they think
❑ Making judgements and decisions informed by reason or evidence

Enquiry skills

❑ Asking relevant questions
❑ Posing and defining problems
❑ Planning what to do
❑ Thinking how to research
❑ Predicting outcomes
❑ Anticipating consequences
❑ Testing conclusions
❑ Improving ideas

Creative thinking skills

❑ Generating and extending ideas
❑ Hypothesising
❑ Applying imagination
❑ Looking for alternative, innovative outcomes

Evaluation skills

❑ Evaluating information
❑ Judging the value of what the learner reads, hears and does
❑ Developing criteria for judging the value of their own and others' work or ideas

Points to consider

There are some important issues to consider as to how the teaching of thinking skills can be implemented into an already crowded timetable.

❑ **How do we create the opportunities for children to acquire and apply these skills?**
❑ **How do we promote these skills in all areas of the curriculum?**
❑ **Are these the only thinking skills we should be teaching in school?**
❑ **How do we take into account the range of learning styles in each class or group?**
❑ **How do we take into account children's own preferred learning styles?**

❑ **Do we need to provide structures and tools to facilitate the acquisition of these skills?**
❑ **How do we make these skills explicit to our learners?**
❑ **How do we assess the progress of children in acquiring and applying these skills?**

Embedding thinking skills in the curriculum

Teachers need to look at the individual National Curriculum subject booklets to find explicit references to the key skills as they relate to each subject. In these booklets there are sections 'Promoting key skills through' … history, or art and so on. In these sections there are suggestions as to the possible opportunities for children to develop the key skills. It should be noted that there are no specific references to them within the programmes of study. This means that schools will have to plan for them carefully and make them explicit within their own schemes of work. We shall be examining the issue of planning in detail in Chapter 3.

There is a similar approach to thinking skills. Under the section 'Promoting other aspects of the curriculum' in the subject booklets there is a short reference to providing opportunities to promote thinking skills. There are a small number of suggested contexts in which thinking skills can be used.

The danger of embedding these skills in something as complex as a school curriculum is that they can become lost and forgotten. Thinking skills and the key skills should be made explicit within schemes of work and particularly within teachers' daily/weekly planning. By making them explicit there is less likelihood they will be overlooked, and clearly defined criteria for assessment can be identified. All planning should begin with identifying the thinking skills to be promoted, used, learned or taught in any learning situation.

Managing thinking in the classroom

In this chapter we shall be examining some practical approaches to the way we as teachers can manage the development of children's thinking and learning.

We shall consider the following.
❑ The role of the school's Teaching and Learning Policy.
❑ The structure of a lesson and the factors that influence the way we plan them.
❑ Managing groups and the learning environment.
❑ Motivating learners to think.
❑ Thinking frames.

The role of the school's Teaching and Learning Policy

If we accept that schools should be explicitly teaching children to become more effective thinkers, to learn meaningfully, to think flexibly and to make reasoned judgements, then they must be taught explicitly how to do it. If we aim to do this in a structured way and to place thinking at the heart of every lesson or learning opportunity then this must be a cornerstone of the school's Teaching and Learning Policy. This policy should state clearly how the school would enable learners to become effective thinkers.

Does your school have a Teaching and Learning Policy, and does it make explicit reference to the development of children's thinking?

We would suggest that the policy should contain references to the following:

❑ Aims of quality teaching
❑ Aims of quality learning
❑ Principles of teaching
❑ Principles of learning
❑ Strategies for the development of thinking skills
❑ Strategies for the planning of thinking opportunities/ activities
❑ Guidelines for fostering a sense of achievement
❑ Strategies for making learning/thinking stimulating

It is only by having a coherent policy and a consistent approach to the teaching of thinking throughout the school that children will be able to reach their potential. The school must ensure that there is continuity and progression for all children.

When managing thinking within the classroom the teacher must be aware of the following principles:

1 Focusing on thinking skills in the classroom supports active cognitive processing, which makes for better learning. It equips the learner to go beyond the information given, to deal systematically yet flexibly with new problems and situations, to adopt a critical attitude to information and argument as well as to communicate effectively.

2 High-quality thinking requires teachers to design or use learning tasks that have a degree of open-endedness in order that learners can impose meaning or make judgements.

3 Learners must be given the time and opportunity to talk about thinking strategies and processes, to make their thought processes more explicit and to reflect on their own strategies.

4 As children bring their own conceptions into the classroom, teachers must introduce new knowledge and alternative strategies for thinking through informed instruction, practical activities, dialogue, reflection and discussion.

5 There needs to be a culture within the classroom (and school) that promotes an open-minded attitude about the nature of knowledge and thinking, and the creation of an atmosphere where talking about thinking – questioning, predicting, contradicting, doubting – is not only tolerated but actively pursued.

6 Teachers should aim to overcome the tendency for haste in thinking by emphasising the need to take time to reflect, puzzle and think things through.

7 Learning is an active, not passive, activity; therefore there must be direct learner involvement.

8 There is a natural vocabulary associated with thinking and this must be modelled and encouraged.

The structure of a lesson

Teachers should give explicit attention to creative, critical and analytical thinking skills through the identification of thinking objectives as well as subject objectives. These objectives should be shared with the children at the beginning of the lesson and referred to when evaluating the learning with the children. This is becoming common practice in schools, often as part of the plenary session at the end of literacy and numeracy lessons.

There are four stages in a typical 'infused' lesson.

1 Generating the interest of the children in both the thinking skill and the subject matter, and sharing the objectives of the lesson.
2 Using 'thinking frames' and 'graphic organizers' in the study of the subject context.
3 Metacognitive discussion reflecting on how the thinking skill was applied.
4 Considering the possibilities for transferring and applying the acquired thinking skill to other areas or situations.

This is a simple structure that both teachers and learners can quickly become familiar with. The skill of the teacher is to make each section stimulating and meaningful for the children. When planning lessons the teacher will need to take account of a variety of factors if they are to enable the children to learn effectively and make progress.

❏ There must be an element of challenge, but not stress, in the lesson.
❏ Take into account the concentration span of the children. It's not as long as you think!
❏ Children learn in different ways. Some will prefer to see information, some will prefer to hear information and some will prefer to be doing things like touching, feeling and making.
❏ The brain needs an adequate amount of oxygen to work effectively and the flow of oxygen is slowed by inactivity, for instance sitting down for too long!
❏ People learn more at the beginning of a lesson.
❏ Children remember the context more than the content of a lesson.
❏ Children learn best when they want to learn. They need to be motivated.

❏ Variety is the spice of life!
❏ Children learn best when they are relaxed, but alert.
❏ Learning is most effective when the learner is actively engaged in doing something.
❏ Learning involves reviewing what has been learnt.

Observe someone's lesson. Focus on:
❏ the structure of the lesson. Did it display any of the four stages of an infused lesson?
❏ the time structure of the lesson and map it out. What did you notice about the quality of engagement and thinking of the children in each section? Was there a peak time? Was there a low point?
❏ the nature of the involvement of the children in the lesson. Were there opportunities for active engagement by the children? Were there times when the children were passively engaged? How did these compare? Was the quality of thinking and learning different at these times?
❏ the opportunities for children to move around and interact with each other. Was there a noticeable difference or improvement in the thinking/learning when this happened?
❏ three or four children. Are they relaxed and alert? Are they challenged but not stressed? How do they compare with each other? Do they display a preferred learning style? Were there opportunities for them to use their preferred learning style?

Share your observations with a colleague. Remember to be sensitive and tactful! Now allow them to observe you! Reflect on your joint findings and plan developmental points for your teaching.

Managing individual learners and groups of learners

Thinking is an activity that individuals do both alone and with others. Your learners will need to experience opportunities for:
❏ solitary thinking
❏ collaborative thinking

It will therefore be necessary for you to consider how you will manage the individual learner working alone and the learner who is engaged in learning in partnership with others. Some of the activities in this book require time and space for individuals to think alone and others require the learner to be collaborating with others, thereby necessitating the provision of the environment in which to do this most effectively.

Solitary thinking

A solitary learner will require ample time to engage in the set task, confident in the knowledge that they will not be interrupted or disturbed by unnecessary distractions. This is best achieved by informing them of the time allotted to the task. Working to a deadline can sharpen the learning process as long as the time allowed is realistic. There needs to be an element of challenge to avoid surplus time in which the learner could become distracted. Judging the correct amount of time for a learning activity, especially if it focuses on thinking, is not easy at first but you will become more confident and accurate as you become more experienced. We must not forget, either, that each individual or class is different and you should use the suggested timescales on the activities as guidance only. It may be that the time you have set is too short or too long. You will need to monitor the activity carefully and be flexible and ready to amend the time if required. Teaching thinking is a very interactive activity and you will be listening and talking to children throughout the lesson, questioning and probing gently to clarify and evaluate the thinking. As you are doing this you will be able to judge whether the time allotted is sufficient or needs amending.

If we are aiming for independent learners then we must allow them to think independently, and to have the time for personalised and internalised thinking.

The solitary learner also requires space. This may seem like an obvious statement but providing the right sort of space can be problematic. Spend a few moments creating a mental picture of your classroom. Picture the seating arrangements, the placement of the furniture and the black/whiteboard. Now imagine yourself as one of your children and that you have been asked to spend ten minutes thinking about how you would change the school uniform. You have to work alone at this stage.

❑ What possible distractions are there?
❑ Where would you prefer to be situated for this activity?
❑ Would you prefer to be static or free to move around?
❑ How will you know how much time you have left?

❑ Would you be able to attract the teacher's attention if you wanted to talk something through or ask a question?
❑ Are there any displays that could assist your thinking?
❑ Have you access to a thinking tool?

Now think about the fact that some of your children will have answered in the same way as you and others will have different preferences. Everyone has their preferred learning style. How can you accommodate the range of learning styles that exists in your class?

As every classroom is different it would be unreasonable to expect us to provide definitive solutions to every possible scenario. However, we would suggest that you consider the following:

❑ how you seat your children
❑ whether it is possible to create an environment and culture where children are able to move around freely, without distracting others, for some activities
❑ how you will move around the class so that you can observe, listen and interact with individual children without you yourself becoming a distraction to others in the class

Collaborative thinking

There will be many occasions when you will want children to think in partnership with others. This may be in pairs, small groups or as a whole class. There is great benefit in thinking along with others. At times the learner may be acting as the innovative thinker driving the process forward towards an outcome; or acting as the critical friend, questioning and probing or pointing out flaws in the thinking being undertaken by others. Once again the key considerations when attempting to create these situations within your class are time and space.

Generally it is fair to say that in these situations the time required is not less than for solitary thinking just because there are more people to share the thinking. In fact it often requires a longer period of time. You should bear this in mind when planning activities that involve groups. There still needs to be an element of challenge in the amount of time you allot in order to focus minds, and yet one still has to be aware of the possible distractions that might occur. It may be that the group diverts away from the task because one or more members of the group are off task and therefore make it much harder for the others to remain on task. It may be that the group moves away from the intended outcome because they are engaged in some meaningful thinking that they have become involved in. They may be so engrossed in what they are doing that they are not aware that they have moved away from the intended outcome. Do they even know what this intended outcome is?

You must ensure each group knows:
❑ what the intended outcome is
❑ what the timescale is for the activity
❑ whether they will be required to 'report back' in some way to the class or other groups

Creating the space to facilitate and enable group thinking is difficult. Your classroom furniture may be versatile enough to allow you to group it or use it in different ways. What does each member of the group require to carry out their role within the group?
❑ Do they need to be able to write or record their thinking and, if so, do they need a table or desk each?
❑ How will they arrange themselves? Will they be in a row, a circle or a semicircle?
❑ Will they be able to arrange themselves or will you direct them as to how they should be arranged?
❑ Is there a culture within your class that allows your learners the freedom to choose?
❑ Do they need to be sitting on chairs or could they sit on the floor or on beanbags?
❑ Do they need to be sitting at all, or could they be standing or moving around?

You will need to be in a position to interact with the group(s) in order to move the thinking forward or clarify the thinking that has occurred so far, and evaluate the thinking outcomes of the group.
❑ How will you arrange each group so that you can move between them observing closely, listening and interacting when appropriate?
❑ How will you be able to judge the amount and quality of each individual's contribution?

A simple way to do this is to ensure that you are able to move around the perimeter of the room thereby giving yourself easy access to the outside groups. At the same time allow sufficient space to move in between groups and to reach the central groups.

Consider the role of the groups. Sometimes each group may be expected to reach an outcome that is independent of the other groups and therefore you will require no interaction between them. At other times each group may be required to contribute something to a whole class outcome, such as how the school uniform could be improved. One group could be considering colours, another the sweatshirts, another the school logo or badge, another PE kit and so on.

Clearly there will be a need at some point for each group to share their ideas with the class or other groups.
❑ How will they present these?
❑ Will they be able to select their own form of presentation or will you as the teacher direct them to use a common format?
❑ How much time will each group need?
❑ How will you need to physically arrange the room and the groups?
❑ Have you allowed enough time? How much noise will you tolerate from each group as they engage in their group task?

There are several techniques that we can use when expecting groups or individuals to feed their ideas into a larger group.
❑ Ask each group to prioritise their contributions and to give their 'star' idea when it's their turn, so that you begin with a collection of the 'cream' of their thinking.
❑ Ask each group to record their ideas on a large piece of paper and post these around the room. Each group can then move from display to display and give their comments at a plenary session. Or ask each group after they have posted their paper to give a two-minute summary of the main points.
❑ Each group has a spokesperson who delivers a short summary of the group's thinking. The act of agreeing the key points for the summary is a good thinking activity in itself.

❑ Mix the groups up and ask the children to tell each other about what they have been thinking and their outcome, and record the things that are common to all groups and the things that are different.

The key is to establish a culture within the class/school that promotes the notion of 'flexibility' and 'fit for the purpose'. Children should be comfortable with the idea that the place of learning is one where it is acceptable to change things around depending on the activity. They should be comfortable within it and able to function effectively whatever the learning task/activity is.

Motivating learners to think

Teachers often naturally assume that if a child is engaged in a set task then they must be thinking. This may be the case but we must ask ourselves some key questions about the thinking that is taking place.

❑ Does the task result in the learner using a range of thinking skills or a particular skill?

❑ Does the task enable the learner to apply and consolidate previously acquired thinking skills?

❑ Is the learner engaged in low-level thinking that does not represent a real challenge and does not move the thinking process forward?

❑ Does the task lead the learner to a sense of satisfaction?

We all know of learners who 'do their work' quickly and with little, if any, fuss. It may be beautifully presented but actually demonstrates a very narrow band of thinking or thinking that is at a level below their potential. Their perception of themselves may be that they are good students and are doing well at school. They may have deliberately chosen to work at a level that is just sufficient to complete the task satisfactorily, without breaking out into a 'thinking sweat'. Clearly these are children who are underachieving. There are many who 'opt out' of tasks because they have low self-esteem about their capabilities, or are lacking in confidence or encouragement. There are those who consciously decide not to do more than the minimum requirement, or whose teachers have too low expectations of their pupils. These learners need to be motivated to expand and develop their thinking.

How do you and your school motivate learners to think?

The key to motivating learners to think and reflect upon their thinking is to make the thinking

❑ stimulating
❑ challenging
❑ intrinsically rewarding
❑ satisfying

Below are some tips that we have found effective. These are not intended to be a definitive list but should be used as a means of generating your own thinking and discussions about how you motivate the thinking of all your learners. Other suggestions can be found in the teacher pages accompanying every activity in the second section of this book.

❑ Make a lively start to the lesson.

❑ Use the natural and topical interests of the children as contexts for thinking.

❑ Engage the learner in active learning (doing) whenever possible.

❑ Create opportunities that allow children to make choices and to develop their own ideas.

❑ Take the learning opportunity (lesson) out of the classroom and into the world the children inhabit for the majority of their lives, or to a new place/situation which will provide new experiences.

❑ Use drama/role-play to allow children to use their imaginations.

❑ Keep the pace of the lesson lively, but not so rushed that the children don't have time to finish the task, revise or reflect.

❑ Use a variety of teaching strategies to cater for different learning styles.

❑ Encourage children to talk about their thinking.

❑ Celebrate and praise children when they display original or effective thinking.

❑ Make thinking fun.

❑ Play thinking games such as those that require children to make connections/associations between objects/items.

❑ Play memory games.

❑ Play strategy games.

❑ Play team games, especially those that require strategies/tactics.

❑ Provide lots of opportunities for children to talk about their ideas and opinions, and value their contributions.

❑ Allow the children to design some thinking activities themselves.

❑ Create thinking challenges and reward all contributors. For example, challenging the children to think of as many uses as possible for a colander (or any other household object). Why not ask the children to think of their own challenges to set the class?

❑ Acknowledge and celebrate progress in thinking and explain why the thinking demonstrates progress.

❑ Encourage parents to become involved in their child's thinking. Create opportunities/challenges for children to do at home that require parents' involvement. For example, joint design projects, playing strategy games or planning a day out. (Be sensitive to those children who may be disadvantaged in this area.)

Assessing thinking

'Can thinking be assessed?' is one of the most frequently asked questions by teachers. Answers to this question promise insights into the very mechanics of learning; a sort of Holy Grail for educators.

There are three distinct avenues for assessing thinking. These avenues give us opportunities to access metacognition (the ability to think about thinking and learning). They are:

1 Through children's articulation of processes undertaken.
2 Through an analysis of judgements made.
3 Through observational evidence in the application of thinking.

Teachers and children can benefit greatly from creating space and time in children's learning for encouraging self-reflection on processes of thinking. The most powerful questions to open the doors to thinking are 'How?' and 'Why?'; they are, of course, the hardest questions to answer but the ones that give us greater insight into processes of thinking.

Thinking is a process. This implies movement from one piece of information to another. 'How did you get from there to here?' and 'How did you decide that?' are questions that open up access to the process of thinking.

Children's articulation of thinking processes

By focusing on the 'thinking journey' rather than the 'destination', teachers will gain greater insight into how the learning is operating and the thinking skills used. It is essentially about the quality of questioning and the ability to listen closely to children's responses. In the all-too-busy life of the classroom, it is easy to take the quick route of closed questioning for quick responses. They offer little to us except a quick overview of outcomes. The skilled teacher will build in opportunities for reflection and articulation of the 'How' of learning and thinking.

In the Cognitive Classroom Project one teacher built up a wall display over a school year showing the 'Seven Keys to Thinking' which were the children's own insights into how thinking worked. 'Sometimes you have to think of lots of ways to do something before you choose the best one. The first one may not be the best,' was one contribution from a Year 5 child. In another classroom the pupils kept a 'Thinking and Learning Diary' to record at the end of a day how they learned and what sort of thinking they used. In one school, a Year 4 teacher and her children designed a 'thinking house', where they could go in pairs or small groups to think and discuss. The tiles of the house (a very large cardboard packing carton) were made from sticky note sheets, each with something children had written about thinking.

Teachers have to make space for the exploration that is thinking. Acceptance that in an argument both parties can be right and that it is in the exploration of differing perceptions that thinking is exposed, is a useful classroom culture to develop. Children would learn more about empathy and their own thinking processes in this way.

It is possible to record key pointers by noting down specific references that individual children make over a term concerning their own articulation of thinking processes. These need only be brief phrases or short sentences but will quickly build to produce a profile of thinking characteristics. Each quote will give an insight into how the child is thinking and will be a valuable piece of formative information.

Analysis of judgements

Another approach to assessing thinking is through an analysis of how children make judgements. Some years ago, Professor E A Peel researched the nature of judgement making. The Cognitive Research Trust used this as a basis for the trial development of tests of thinking skills by identifying children's responses to questions that did not hold enough information for a full judgement to be made. For example:

Cows eat grass and give milk. Goats eat grass and give milk. Are cows like goats?

The preparedness of children to make a judgement in such situations depended on their ability to see 'beyond the information given'. Responses were analysed in one of five types:

+ where a positive judgement is made – 'Yes, they are alike.'

– where a negative judgement is made – 'No, they are not alike.'

⊕ where a positive judgement is made but there is realisation that information is incomplete, for example 'Yes, but they are different sizes.'

⊖ where a negative judgement is made but there is realisation that information is incomplete, for example 'No, but they do eat the same food.'

○ where the lack of sufficient information is fully appreciated and there is a reluctance to make a judgement, for example 'It depends. In some ways they are; in some ways they are not.'

The proportion of responses ⊕ ⊖ and ○ was noted and then, after a period of time in which thinking skills were specifically developed, a parallel retest was undertaken. Research showed an increase in the proportion of such responses indicating a probable increase in the ability of the children to see beyond the information given; in other words to think.

It is possible to develop such tests to identify how judgements are being made, and by assessing responses from children as they develop their thinking skills.

Observational analysis of applications

It is possible to identify characteristics of thinking from observation of children's responses to a problem-solving situation. The following questions can act as an *aide-mémoire* for such a process:

❑ What information is the child using?
❑ How is the child using this information?
❑ How is the child moving from one idea to the next?
❑ What part do guesswork and random thought play?
❑ What other thinking strategies does the child use?
❑ Can the child synthesise outcomes and make a judgement?

The value of observation of a child undertaking a task cannot be overstated. Again it is important in terms of classroom organisation and management for learning that time is built in for such formative assessments to be made formally or informally. Too often our focus as teachers is on managing the activity rather than on observing how children are thinking and learning. Where a teacher is systematically developing children's independence in learning, there is a greater opportunity for observational formative assessment. Ask yourself the questions, 'Are the children I teach too dependent on my organisation of learning?' and 'How can I increase their independence to reduce my organisational and directional time?'

It is a provocative thought to suggest that in organising and simplifying learning for the benefit of our children we may, in fact, be protecting them from the complexity of real life learning. Perhaps we should increase the challenges we present to them and build supportive and constructive relationships with them as we, together, explore the complexities that are learning in our ever more sophisticated culture.

Certainly the use of observational analysis can be extremely powerful in identifying thinking processes at work. Any subsequent feedback and dialogue with a child can make explicit the awareness of thinking processes upon which the child can build their future thinking and learning.

****

It may be interpreted from this section that we have an acute awareness of the lack of transferable value of information gained from traditional 'reasoning tests' in increasing a child's thinking skills. We believe that, at best, they provide an indicator of a child's ability to undertake a test of reasoning.

As our awareness of how the brain works increases, the complexity of our society snowballs and the role of information management (rather than acquisition) becomes more prevalent, the role of thinking becomes more important. Thus there is a need for us to explore and develop further strategies for assessing thinking skills in the future.

Planning for thinking skills

Thinking skills should not be treated as an additional subject to be taught but as a set of skills that enable learners to become better learners within each subject area. By improving the thinking one improves the learning. There needs to be the opportunity to teach these skills and for the learner to practise, consolidate and apply them. They can be taught separately or as part of other curriculum work. The activities that follow are a means of introducing each skill using non-subject specific contexts. It will be necessary to provide further opportunities in a range of subject contexts in order for the pupils to develop them further.

To enable teachers to include thinking skills in their school schemes of work we have identified where in the Programmes of Study for each subject each set of skills can be included. These references are contained in a set of planning tables.

Guidance on using the planning tables

Each subject in the National Curriculum has an accompanying booklet that:
❑ sets out the legal requirements of the National Curriculum
❑ provides information to help teachers implement it in their schools

Within each booklet is a section 'Learning across the National Curriculum' which contains a subsection 'Promoting other aspects of the curriculum'. One of the aspects it refers to is thinking skills. Below are all these sections compiled into one easy reference. This is followed by a series of planning tables, which identify specific references to the different thinking skills in each subject.

SUBJECT	OPPORTUNITIES TO PROMOTE THINKING SKILLS
ENGLISH	• Reading, viewing and discussing texts which present issues and relationships. • Developing pupils' ability to put their point of view, question, argue and discuss. • Evaluating critically what they hear, read and view. • Being competent users of English to aid decision making.
MATHS	• Developing pupils' problem-solving skills and deductive reasoning.
SCIENCE	• Engaging in the process of scientific enquiry.
HISTORY	• Work involving processing and evaluating information. • Describing and explaining events and actions. • Carrying out investigations of past events.
GEOGRAPHY	• The process of geographical enquiry. • Evaluating information and reflecting on own work.
DESIGN AND TECHNOLOGY	• Identifying relevant sources of information. • Developing criteria for designs to guide thinking.
PE	• Considering information and concepts. • Critically evaluating aspects of performance. • Generating and expressing own ideas and opinions about tactics, strategy and composition.
ART AND DESIGN	• Asking and answering questions about starting points for work. • Exploring and developing ideas. • Collecting and organising visual and other information to develop work. • Investigating possibilities. • Reviewing what has been done. • Adapting and refining work. • Making reasoned judgements and decisions about how to develop ideas.
MUSIC	• Analysing and evaluating music. • Adopting and developing musical ideas. • Working creatively, reflectively and spontaneously.

Information-processing skills

❏ Locating and collecting relevant information
❏ Sorting
❏ Classifying
❏ Sequencing
❏ Comparing and contrasting
❏ Analysing part/whole relationships

SUBJECT	ACTIVITIES
ENGLISH	*Reading for information* **Key Stage 1** • Using the organisational features of non-fiction texts to find information (2a) • Understanding that texts about the same topic may contain different information or present similar information in different ways (2b) • Using reference material for different purposes (2c) **Key Stage 2** • Distinguishing between fact and opinion (3f) • Considering an argument critically (3g) **Generic information-processing skills (not identified within the English programmes of study)** • Generating questions and using literacy skills to locate information enabling answers to be found • Suggesting and selecting appropriate sources • Interrogating information contained in charts and tables and identifying and using the relevant information • Examining similar information presented in different ways and giving reasons for which is the most useful • Examining information and making deductions from this through sorting, classifying, sequencing, comparing and contrasting, and analysing relationships
MATHS	*Processing, representing and interpreting data* **Key Stage 1** • Solving a relevant problem by using simple lists, tables and charts to sort, classify and organise information (5a) **Key Stage 2** **Generic information-processing skills (not identified within the maths programmes of study)** • Generating their own questions or suggest areas for exploration and use simple lists, tables and charts to sort, classify and organise information • Collecting everyday examples of charts, tables and lists and identifying their strengths and weaknesses, giving reasons for ideas The use of mathematical skills complements the thinking skill of information processing, and opportunities should be found to use these in other areas of the curriculum.

Information-processing skills

SCIENCE	*Sc1* **Key Stage 1** *Ideas and evidence in science* • Collecting evidence by making observations and measurements (1) *Investigative skills* • Using first-hand experience and simple information sources to answer questions (2b) • Recognising when a test or comparison is not fair (2d) • Using the senses to make and record observations and measurements (2f) • Communicating what happened in a variety of ways (2g) • Making simple comparisons and identifying simple patterns or associations (2h) • Comparing what happened with what was expected would happen, and trying to explain it (2i) **Key Stage 2** • Considering what sources of evidence to use to answer questions (2b) • Making systematic observations and measurements, including the use of ICT for data logging (2f) • Checking observations and measurements by repeating them where appropriate (2g) • Using a wide range of methods to communicate data in an appropriate and systematic manner (2h) • Making comparisons and identifying simple patterns or associations in their own observations and measurements or other data (2i)
HISTORY	*History provides opportunities to promote thinking skills through work on processing and evaluating information.* *Historical enquiry* **Key Stage 1** • Finding out about the past from a range of information (4a) **Key Stage 2** • Finding out about the events, people and changes studied from an appropriate range of sources of information, including ICT sources (4a) • Selecting and recording information relevant to the focus of an enquiry (4b) • Organising and communicating • Recalling, selecting and organising historical information (5a)
GEOGRAPHY	*Geography provides opportunities to promote thinking skills through helping learners to evaluate information and reflect on their own work.* *Geographical enquiry and skills* **Key Stage 1** • Using fieldwork skills to collect and record information (2b) • Using secondary sources of information (2d) **Key Stage 2** • Collecting and recording evidence (1b) • Analysing evidence and drawing conclusions (1c) • Using appropriate fieldwork techniques and instruments to collect information (2b) • Using secondary sources of information (2d) • Using ICT to record and analyse information and data (2f)

Information processing skills

DESIGN AND TECHNOLOGY	*Design and technology provides the opportunity to promote thinking skills through learners identifying relevant sources of information.* ***Developing, planning and communicating ideas*** **Key Stage 1** • Generating ideas by drawing on their and others' experiences and on information (1a) **Key Stage 2** • Generating ideas for products using information from a number of sources, including ICT based sources (1a)
PHYSICAL EDUCATION	*PE provides the opportunity to promote thinking skills through learners considering information that suits the different activities.* *There are no direct references to information-processing skills in the PE programmes of study.*
ART AND DESIGN	*Art and design provides the opportunity to promote thinking skills through learners collecting and organising visual and other information and using this to develop their work.* *There are no direct references to information processing skills in the Art and design programmes of study, but there are opportunities to:* • Compare and contrast
ICT	*ICT provides opportunities to promote thinking skills through helping learners identify relevant sources of information.* ***Finding things out*** **Key Stage 1** • Gathering information from a range of sources (1a) • Entering and storing information in a variety of forms (1b) • Retrieving information that has been stored (1c) **Key Stage 2** • Talking about what information is needed and how to find and use it (1a) • Preparing information for development using ICT, including selecting suitable sources, finding information, classifying it and checking it for accuracy (1b) • Interpreting information, checking it (and thinking about what might happen if it were wrong or had omissions. See Enquiry skills) (1c) ***Developing ideas and making things happen*** **Key Stage 1** • Selecting from and adding to information they have retrieved (2b) **Key Stage 2** • Organising and reorganising texts, tables, images and sounds to develop and refine ideas (2a) ***Exchanging and sharing ideas*** **Key Stage 1** • Sharing ideas by presenting information in a variety of forms (3a) **Key Stage 2** • Sharing and exchanging information in a variety of forms (3a) • Being sensitive to the needs of the audience, and thinking about the content and quality when communicating information (3b)
MUSIC	*There are no direct references to information-processing skills in the programmes of study, but there are opportunities to:* • Compare and contrast

Reasoning skills

❑ Giving reasons for actions and opinions
❑ Drawing inferences
❑ Making deductions
❑ Using precise language to explain thinking
❑ Making judgements and decisions informed by reasons or evidence

SUBJECT	ACTIVITIES
ENGLISH	**En 1** *Group discussion and interaction* **Key Stage 1** • Giving reasons for opinions and actions (3e) **Key Stage 2** • Making reasoned, evaluative comments as the discussion moves towards conclusions or actions (3b) • Qualifying or justifying what they think after listening to others' questions or accounts (3c) **En 2** *Literature* **Key Stage 1** • Expressing preferences, giving reasons (3c) **Key Stage 2** • Understanding texts (2) Using inference and deduction (2a) Looking for meaning beyond the literal (2b) • Reading for information (3) Considering an argument critically (3g) • Literature (4) Expressing preferences (4g) • Non-fiction and non-literary texts (5) Identifying words associated with reason, persuasion, argument, explanation (5b)
MATHS	*Maths provides opportunities to promote thinking skills through deductive reasoning.* **Ma 2** *Reasoning* **Key Stage 1** • Presenting results in an organised way (1g) • Understanding a general statement and investigating whether particular cases match it (1h) • Explaining methods used and reasoning when solving problems involving number and data (1i) • Solving numerical problems • Checking answers and explaining methods or reasoning (4b) **Key Stage 2** • Developing logical thinking and explaining reasoning (1k) • Solving numerical problems • Choosing and using an appropriate way to calculate and explaining methods and reasoning (4b)

	Ma 3 *Reasoning* **Key Stage 1** • Using mathematical communication and explanation skills (1f) **Key Stage 2** • Using mathematical reasoning to explain features of shape and space (1h) **Ma 4** *Reasoning* **Key Stage 2** • Explaining and justifying methods and reasoning (1h)
SCIENCE	*There are no direct references to reasoning skills in the programmes of study; however, there are clear opportunities for learners to give reasons for their actions and opinions and make deductions and judgements in their investigative activities.*
HISTORY	*History provides opportunities to promote thinking skills through describing and explaining events and actions.* ***Knowledge and understanding of events, people and changes in the past*** **Key Stage 1** • Recognising why people did things, why events happened and what happened as a result (2a) **Key Stage 2** • Identifying and describing reasons for, and results of, historical events, situations, and changes in periods studied (2c) • Making links between the main events, situations and changes within and across the different periods and societies studied (2d) ***Historical interpretation*** **Key Stage 2** • Recognising that the past is represented and interpreted in different ways, and to give reasons for this (3)
GEOGRAPHY	***Geographical enquiry and skills*** **Key Stage 1** • Expressing own views about people, places and environments (1c) **Key Stage 2** • Identifying and explaining different views that people, including themselves, hold about topical geographical issues (1d) • Using decision-making skills (2g) ***Knowledge and understanding of places*** • Explaining why places are like they are (3d) • Describing and explaining how and why places are similar to and different from other places (3f) ***Knowledge and understanding of patterns and processes*** • Recognising and explaining patterns made by individual physical and human features in the environment (4a) • Recognising some physical and human processes and explaining how these can cause changes in places and environments (4b)

Reasoning skills

DESIGN AND TECHNOLOGY	*Developing, planning and communicating ideas* **Key Stage 1** • Talking about their ideas (1c) **Key Stage 2** • Developing ideas and explaining them clearly (1c)
PHYSICAL EDUCATION	*PE provides opportunities to promote thinking skills through generating and expressing own ideas and opinions about tactics, strategy and composition.* *Acquiring and developing skills* **Key Stage 1** • Exploring ideas with increasing understanding (1a) *Selecting and applying skills, tactics and compositional ideas* **Key Stage 1** • Exploring how to choose and apply skills and actions (2a) • Varying performance by using simple tactics (2b) **Key Stage 2** • Planning, using and adapting strategies, tactics and compositional ideas (2a)
ART AND DESIGN	*There are no direct references to reasoning skills in the programmes of study, but there are opportunities to:* • Give reasons for opinions and actions • Use precise language to explain thinking • Make judgements and decisions informed by reasons or evidence
ICT	*There are no direct references to reasoning skills in the programmes of study, but there are opportunities to:* • Give reasons for opinions and actions • Use precise language to explain thinking • Make judgements and decisions informed by reasons or evidence
MUSIC	*There are no direct references to reasoning skills in the programmes of study, but there are opportunities to:* • Give reasons for opinions and actions • Use precise language to explain thinking • Make judgements and decisions informed by reasons or evidence

Enquiry skills

- ❑ Asking relevant questions
- ❑ Posing and defining problems
- ❑ Planning what to do
- ❑ Deciding how to research
- ❑ Predicting outcomes
- ❑ Anticipating consequences
- ❑ Testing conclusions
- ❑ Improving ideas

SUBJECT	ACTIVITIES
ENGLISH	**En 1** *Listening* **Key Stage 1** • Asking questions to clarify understanding (2e) **Key Stage 2** • Asking relevant questions to clarify, extend and follow up ideas (2b) **Key Stage 2** *Group discussion and interaction* • Anticipating consequences to move a discussion forward (3f) **En 2** *Reading for information* **Key Stage 1** • Using reference materials for different purposes (2c) *Literature* • Predicting events in a story (3b) **Key Stage 2** *There are no direct references to enquiry skills in the English programmes of study, but these are generic:* • Asking relevant questions that can be answered using a variety of texts • Planning what to do and how to research
MATHS	**Ma 2** **Key Stage 1** • Identifying what needs to be done when approaching problems involving number (1a) • Developing flexible approaches to problem solving and looking for ways to overcome difficulties (1b) • Deciding which operations and problem-solving strategies to use (1c) • Choosing sensible calculation methods to solve number problems (4a) **Key Stage 2** • Breaking down more complex problems into simpler steps before attempting a solution (1b) • Finding different ways to approach a problem in order to overcome any difficulties (1d) • Choosing suitable number operations to solve a given problem (4a) **Ma 3** **Key Stage 1** • Trying different approaches and finding ways of overcoming difficulties when solving problems (1a) • Selecting appropriate equipment to solve problems (1b) • Making predictions about simple patterns and relationships (1e)

Enquiry skills

	Ma3 **Key Stage 2** • Selecting and using appropriate calculation skills (1b) • Approaching problems flexibly, including trying alternative approaches to overcome difficulties (1c) **Ma 4** **Key Stage 2** • Approaching problems flexibly, including trying alternative approaches to overcome difficulties (1b) • Selecting and using appropriate calculation skills to solve problems involving data (1d) • Drawing conclusions from statistics and graphs (2f)
SCIENCE	*Science provides opportunities to promote thinking skills through learners engaging in the process of scientific enquiry.* **Sc1** ***Ideas and evidence in science*** **Key Stage 1** • When trying to answer a question, learners should be taught that it is important to collect evidence by making observations and measurements (1) ***Investigative skills*** **Key Stage 1** • Asking questions and deciding how to find answers to them (2a) • Answering questions by using first-hand experience and simple information sources (2b) • Thinking about what might happen before deciding what to do (2c) • Comparing what happened with what was expected, and trying to explain it by drawing on their knowledge and understanding (2i) **Key Stage 2** • Asking questions that can be investigated scientifically and deciding how to find answers (2a) • Asking questions and considering what sources of information, including first-hand experiences and a range of other sources, will be used to answer them (2b) • Thinking about what might happen or trying things out when deciding what to do (2c) • Drawing conclusions by using observations, measurements or other data (2j) • Deciding whether these conclusions agree with any predictions made and/or whether they enable other predictions to be made (2k) • Using scientific knowledge and understanding to explain observations, measurements or other data or conclusions (2l)
HISTORY	*History provides opportunities to promote thinking skills through carrying out investigations of past events.* ***Historical enquiry*** **Key Stage 1** • Asking and answering questions about the past (4b) **Key Stage 2** • Deciding how to find out about the events, people and changes studied (4a) • Asking and answering questions, and selecting and recording information relevant to the focus of the enquiry (4b)

Enquiry skills

GEOGRAPHY	Geography provides opportunities to promote thinking skills through emphasis on the process of geographical enquiry.
	Geographical enquiry skills
	Key Stage 1
	• Asking geographical questions (1a)
	Key Stage 2
	• Asking geographical questions (1a)
	• Analysing evidence and drawing conclusions (1c)
	Knowledge and understanding of places
	Key Stage 2
	• Identifying how places may change in the future (3e)
DESIGN AND TECHNOLOGY	**Developing, planning and communicating ideas**
	Key Stage 1
	• Planning by suggesting what to do next as ideas develop (1d)
	Key Stage 2
	• Planning what to do, suggesting a series of actions and alternatives, if needed (1c)
ART AND DESIGN	Art and design provides opportunities to promote thinking skills through encouraging learners to ask and answer questions about starting points for their work and investigate possibilities.
	Exploring and developing ideas
	Key Stage 1
	• Asking and answering questions about the starting points for their work (1b)
	Key Stage 2
	• Questioning and making thoughtful observations about starting points (1b)
ICT	**Key Stage 1**
	Developing ideas and making things happen
	• Planning and giving instructions to make things happen (2c)
	• Trying things out and exploring what happens in real and imaginary situations (2d)
	Key Stage 2
	Finding things out
	• Thinking about what might happen if information has errors or omissions (1c)
	Developing ideas and making things happen
	• Developing and refining ideas by bringing together, organising and reorganising text, tables, images and sound as appropriate (2a)
	• Testing, improving and refining sequences of instructions to make things happen and responding to them (2b)
	• Using simulations and exploring models to answer 'What if… ?' questions (2c)
MUSIC	There are no direct references to enquiry skills in the programmes of study, but there are opportunities to:
	• Develop ideas

Creative thinking skills

❑ Generating and extending ideas
❑ Hypothesising
❑ Applying imagination
❑ Looking for alternative innovative outcomes

SUBJECT	ACTIVITIES
ENGLISH	**En 1** **Key Stage 1** *Group discussion and interaction* • Extending ideas in the light of discussion **Key Stage 2** *Listening* • Asking relevant questions to clarify, extend and follow up ideas (2b) *Group discussion and interaction* • Considering alternatives to move a discussion forward (3f) *Drama* • Using drama to convey ideas (4b) **En 2** *Literature* **Key Stage 1** • Responding imaginatively in different ways to what is read (3f) **Key Stage 2** • Responding imaginatively to texts (4h) **En 3** *Composition* **Key Stage 1** • Putting ideas into sentences (1c) *Planning and drafting* • Developing ideas on paper (2b) The range of purposes for writing should include: • Creating imaginary worlds **Key Stage 2** The range of purposes for writing should include: • Imagining and exploring feelings and ideas
MATHS	*There are no specific references to creative thinking skills in the maths curriculum. However, there will be opportunities for generating and extending ideas in problem solving. Often maths will be used in other problem-solving contexts to generate and extend ideas and to look for alternative innovative outcomes.*

Creative thinking skills

SCIENCE	**Sc1** **Key Stage 2** *Ideas and evidence in science* • Thinking creatively to try and explain how living things and non-living things work, and to establish links between causes and effects (1a) • Testing ideas using evidence from observation and measurement (1b)
HISTORY	*There are no specific references to creative thinking skills in the history curriculum. However, there will be opportunities for generating and extending ideas when thinking about events in the past, and for thinking about possible alternative outcomes to an event in the past.*
GEOGRAPHY	**Key Stage 2** *Knowledge and understanding of patterns and places* • Explaining how some physical and human processes can cause changes in places and environments (4b) *Knowledge and understanding of environmental change and sustainable development* • Recognising how decisions about places and environments affect the future quality of people's lives (5a) Both of these provide opportunities to look for alternative innovative outcomes, and to hypothesise about life in the future.
DESIGN AND TECHNOLOGY	*Developing, planning and communicating ideas* **Key Stage 1** • Generating ideas by drawing on own and others' experiences (1a) • Developing ideas by shaping materials and putting together components (1b) • Talking about ideas (1c) **Key Stage 2** • Generating ideas for products after thinking about who will use them and what they will be used for (1a) • Developing ideas and explaining them clearly, putting together a list of what they want their design to achieve (1b)
PE	*Acquiring and developing skills* **Key Stage 1** • Exploring ideas with increasing understanding (1a) *Dance activities* **Key Stage 1** • Using movement imaginatively (6a) • Creating and performing dances (6c) • Expressing and communicating ideas and feelings (6d) **Key Stage 2** • Creating and performing dances (6a) *Games activities* **Key Stage 1** Playing simple games that they have made (7c) **Key Stage 2** Making up games (7a)

Creative thinking skills

	Gymnastic activities **Key Stage 1** • Creating and performing short sequences (8d) **Key Stage 2** • Creating and performing sequences (8a) ***Athletic activities*** **Key Stage 2** • Designing challenges and competitions (10a)
ART AND DESIGN	***Exploring and developing ideas*** **Key Stage 1** • Developing their ideas (1b) ***Investigating and making art, craft and design*** **Key Stage 1** • Representing ideas and feelings (2c) **Key Stage 2** • Developing their ideas (1c) ***Investigating and making art, craft and design*** **Key Stage 2** • Using a variety of methods and approaches to communicate ideas and feelings (2c)
ICT	*There are no direct references to creative skills in the programmes of study, but there are clear opportunities for:* • Generating and extending ideas • Applying imagination • Looking for alternative innovative outcomes
MUSIC	*There are no direct references to creative skills in the programmes of study, but there are clear opportunities for:* • Generating and extending ideas • Applying imagination • Looking for alternative innovative outcomes

Evaluation skills

❑ Evaluating information
❑ Judging the value of what's read, heard and done
❑ Developing criteria for judging the value of own work and others' work or ideas

SUBJECT	ACTIVITIES
ENGLISH	**En 1** *Knowledge skills and understanding* **Key Stage 1** • Commenting constructively on drama watched or taken part in (4c) **Key Stage 2** • Evaluating own speech and reflect on how it varies (1f) • Identifying the gist of an argument or key points in a discussion and evaluating what is heard (2a) • Evaluating comments as a discussion moves to conclusions or actions (3b) • Using different ways to help group discussion move forward, including summarising the main points, reviewing what has been said (3f) • Evaluating contributions to the overall effectiveness of drama performances (4d) **En 2** *Literature* **Key Stage 2** • Evaluating ideas and themes that broaden perspectives and extend thinking (4e) *Non-fiction and non-literary texts* • Evaluating different formats, layouts and presentational devices (5f) **En 3** *Planning and drafting* **Key Stage 1** • Planning and reviewing own writing, discussing the quality of what is written (2c) **Key Stage 2** • Revising, changing and improving draft (2c) • Discussing and evaluating own and others' writing (2f)
MATHS	**Ma2** *Using and applying number* **Key Stage 1** • Organising and checking work (1d) • Checking answers are reasonable (4b) • Discussing what has been done (5b) **Key Stage 2** • Checking results (1e) • Refining ways of recording (1f) • Estimating answers and checking results are reasonable by thinking about the context of the problem, and, where necessary, checking accuracy (4c)

	Ma 3 *Problem solving* **Key Stage 2** • Using checking procedures to confirm results are reasonable (1d) **Ma 4** *Problem solving* **Key Stage 2** • Checking results ensuring solutions are reasonable in the context of the problem (1e)
SCIENCE	**Sc 1** *Investigative skills* **Key Stage 1** • Reviewing work and explaining to others what they did (2j) **Key Stage 2** • Checking observations and measurements by repeating where appropriate (2g) • Reviewing own work and work of others and describing its significance and limitations (2m)
HISTORY	*There are no direct references to evaluation skills in the programmes of study, but there are clear opportunities for learners to:* • Evaluate the actions and events of the past • Evaluate historical information • Judge the value of what's read • Develop criteria for judging the value of their and others' work and ideas
GEOGRAPHY	*There are no direct references to evaluation skills in the programmes of study, but there are clear opportunities for learners to:* • Evaluate geographical information • Judge the value of what's read • Develop criteria for judging the value of their and other's work and ideas
DESIGN AND TECHNOLOGY	*Evaluating processes and products* **Key Stage 1** • Talking about own ideas, saying what is liked and disliked (3a) • Identifying what could have been done differently or how work could be improved in the future (3b) **Key Stage 2** • Reflecting on the progress of work, and identifying ways of improving products (3a) • Carrying out appropriate tests before making any improvements (3b) • Evaluating the quality of products (3c)
PE	*Evaluating and improving performance* **Key Stage 1** • Using what has been learnt to improve the quality and control of work (3c) **Key Stage 2** • Identifying what makes a performance better (3a) • Suggesting improvements to performance (3b)

Evaluation skills

ART AND DESIGN	***Evaluating and developing work*** **Key Stage 1** • Reviewing what they and others have done, saying what they think and feel about it (3a) • Identifying what they might change in current work or develop in future work (3b) **Key Stage 2** • Comparing ideas, methods and approaches in their and others' work saying what they think and feel about it (3a) • Adapting work and describing how it might develop further (3b)
ICT	***Reviewing, modifying and evaluating work as it progresses*** **Key Stage 1** • Reviewing what has been done to help develop ideas (4a) • Describing the effects of actions (4b) • Talking about what might be changed in future work (4c) **Key Stage 2** • Reviewing what has been done to help develop ideas (4a) • Describing and talking about the effectiveness of work with ICT, comparing it with other methods and considering the effect it has on others (4b) • Talking about how work could be improved in the future (4c)
MUSIC	***Responding and reviewing*** **Key Stage 1** • Making improvements to work (3b) **Key Stage 2** • Improving own and others' work in relation to its intended effect (3c)

USING THE PLANNING TABLES TO AID MEDIUM-TERM PLANNING

THINKING SKILLS	PoS OBJECTIVE (KNOWLEDGE AND UNDERSTANDING)	ACTIVITY	SUCCESS CRITERIA THE LEARNER IS ABLE TO...
YEAR 1			
YEAR 2			
YEAR 3			
YEAR 4			
YEAR 5			
YEAR 6			

When reviewing or drawing up medium-term plans refer to the tables to identify the thinking skills and the objectives within each subject and decide in which year it will be introduced and taught. Next decide the activity or activities that will be used to develop and apply each skill. Some suggestions for possible activities can be found in the next section of this book. Once this has been done decide how you will know if the learner has been successful. What will they be able to do? This will aid your assessment. Then record your plan using the framework above.

THE FOLLOWING PAGES CONTAIN THUNKS FOR THE THINKING SKILLS AREAS FOR BOTH KEY STAGES ONE AND TWO. BELOW IS AN OVERVIEW OF THE THUNKS, SHOWING THE TITLES AND RELEVANTS SKILLS. **TF** INDICATES THAT THERE IS A PHOTOCOPIABLE THINKING FRAME TO ACCOMPANY THIS ACTIVITY. THESE CAN BE FOUND AT THE BACK OF THE BOOK.

	Thinking skill	No	Key Stage 1 activity	Key Stage 2 activity
Information-processing	Locating and collecting information	1	The jigsaw **TF**	The orchestra
	Sorting information	2	What do we have in common?**TF**	Sort the spellings
	Classifying	3	Name it **TF**	What's on the box?
	Sequencing	4	Getting dressed	Stepping stones **TF**
	Comparing and contrasting	5	Same, similar or different?	Alike and unalike
	Analysing relationships	6	Links **TF**	Pick a card, any card **TF**
Reasoning	Giving reasons for opinions and actions	7	The 'Because' game	Because **TF**
	Making deductions	8	N/A	The time capsule **TF**
	Explaining thinking	9	Leaping from stone to stone **TF**	Leaping from stone to stone **TF**
	Making judgements and decisions informed by reasoning or evidence	10	Decisions, decisions!	Making reasoned decisions
Enquiry	Asking relevant questions	11	What, when, how?	Twenty questions
	Posing and defining problems	12	Problems, problems, problems!	Wheelchair
	Planning what to do	13	Making plans	A day out
	Researching	14	Search it out	When I grow up I want to be …
	Predicting outcomes	15	What happens next?	Crystal ball gazing
	Anticipating consequences	16	N/A	The ripple effect **TF**
	Testing conclusions	17	Sandcastles	Testing conclusions
	Improving ideas	18	Making it better	Playgrounds
Creative thinking	Generating and extending ideas	19	That's a good idea!	Rubbery ideas! **TF**
	Hypothesising	20	I wonder why?	The 'Why?' game
	Applying imagination	21	Toy plays	Concept stories
	Looking for alternative outcomes	22	New animals	What would happen if …?
Evaluation	Evaluating information	23	How good is my information?	How good is my information?
	Judging the value of what is heard, seen and done	24	How good is my work?	How will I know how good my work is? **TF**
	Developing criteria for judging the value of own or others work	25	N/A	Being a guide

Key skills

- Communication
- Working with others
- Problem solving
- Application of number

Subject links

- Geography
- Numeracy

Aim

- To locate and collect information from the immediate environment, such as the school.

Organisation

Pairs

Time

45 minutes

Resources

- 'The planning frame' on page 130

Outcomes

- The children will have created a visual representation of the information collected, and will have developed an understanding of the working parts of a school.

The jigsaw

Task

Ask the children to tell you what they already know about the different parts of the school, such as the headteacher's office. Can they name the parts? Do the names give a clue to the purpose of that part of the school?

What characteristics or features help them to recognise each part, for example a classroom? List the parts and their characteristics on the board.

Next ask the children to work in pairs and explore the school to look for the information needed, for example the number of classrooms and what other rooms or areas there are and what they are used for. The children should keep a tally chart of the information.

The class should then report their findings to the teacher.

Each pair then records their findings on the planning frame (page 130). They can either write or draw pictures to represent each part of the school.

Teaching tip

Encourage the children to use the word 'information' as much as possible. Instead of asking 'What have you found out?' ask 'What information have you found?' Give each pair a simple sheet with boxes marked for different parts of the school; they use these for a tally chart of each part.

Reinforce the concept of the jigsaw as being separate pieces of information which make up a whole picture. In other words when we collect different pieces of information and these are put together we have an overall understanding of something, or a concept.

Extension activities

❑ Give the children a simplified map of the school. Each pair has to identify the different parts of the school on the map. They must then devise a colour key for each part.

❑ Each pair could then use their numeracy skills to record the number of people using each part of the school.

❑ If there is a local shopping area near to the school, the children could collect information about some of the shops. Groups of children could visit a shop (with adult supervision) and collect information about it, such as opening times, what it sells, how old the shop is and how many people work in it. Each group should then draw a picture of their shop and report back to the whole class what information they have collected. All the pictures could then be displayed as a frieze to give an overall impression of the shopping area. Information about each shop could be displayed under each picture.

Assessment

- Assess if the children have been able to identify all the main areas of the school.

- Assess if they understand what the main purpose is of each sort of area.

- Assess if they are able to identify some of the main characteristics of each sort of area, for example classrooms have many tables with chairs around them or offices are much smaller than classrooms.

The assessment can be through scrutiny of the outcomes on the thinking frame, and through careful questioning.

Information-processing skills: Locating and collecting information

Key skills

- Communication
- ICT
- Problem solving

Subject links

- Science
- Music

Aim

- To locate and collect relevant information on the different instruments found in an orchestra.

Organisation

Groups of three

Time

1 hour (access to ICT may need to be spread over a longer period)

Resources

- Information books
- CD-Roms on music/orchestras
- Internet access

Outcomes

- The children will be able to give the names of each instrument in the orchestra and a description of how each one is played.

The orchestra

Task

Provide the children with various resources, such as books, CD-Roms, audio tapes, posters and access to the Internet, that will give them information on the orchestra.

Before using these resources, ask the children to tell you what instruments they already know. Ask them if they know how they are played.

Then ask them to use the central supply of resources to compile a list of the different instruments and a simple description of how each of them is played.

As a plenary ask the groups to feed back to the class on the following:
❑ How did they collect the information?
❑ Which source was most useful?
❑ Which was the quickest way of locating the information?
❑ What literacy skills did they use?

Teaching tip

Ensure that there are sufficient resources available.

Ensure that there are equal opportunities for everyone to use the ICT resources. You may need to organise a rota for each group if you do not have an ICT suite in your school.

To avoid a rush towards the resources and the random grabbing of them, encourage the groups to start by thinking about what sort of resources might be useful to them and how they can quickly determine if a source is going to be useful (title, contents page and index). Also, encourage them to think about what they might do with the information once they have located it. Will they take quick notes, or share the information with the whole group and agree if it is useful and relevant, or will they copy information down verbatim? Will they need access to ICT either to locate the information or to help store it? For instance by scanning a page of a book and printing it out, or saving it to disk?

Extension activities

❑ Once the information is located and collected ask the children to make an audio tape of some of the different instruments and a commentary on how each is played.

❑ Divide the class into groups and allocate one section of the orchestra – the brass section, woodwind, percussion, strings – to each group. The task is for each group to locate and collect information for their section and devise their own way of presenting that information to the whole class (or to another class of younger children). Encourage them to use a multimedia approach to the presentation. After their presentations ask each group why they chose to present it in that way. What was their thinking behind it?

❑ Instead of locating information about the orchestra, the children could find out about different instruments from around the world.

❑ This skill of locating and collecting information can be related to enquiry skills, particularly asking relevant questions. This can be reinforced by asking the children to locate and collect information about their own chosen topic. But before they do they have to pose five questions about that topic that they would like to find the answers to. For example, the topic chosen is the Olympics. They might pose questions such as, 'When did the Olympics begin?' and 'How many sports are there in the Olympics?'

Assessment

• Observation of how children are locating and collecting the information. Is it random 'dipping into' sources of information or are literacy skills such as study skills and using index being used? How are the children organising/managing their search for information?

What do we have in common?

Task

Model the sorting process by using an example set of objects. For example, show the children a set of toy vehicles (cars, lorries, buses and so on). Don't use more than five at this stage. Tell the children you are going to sort them into groups (no more than two groups at this stage) and ask them to help you. When the children are confident, extend the set and the number of subsets.

Then organise the children into pairs and give each pair a set of plastic shapes, the properties of which have been predetermined by you, for example a set containing circles and squares, or all rectangles but two different colours.

The children might like to use the thinking frame on page 131 and draw or write the name of each shape in the appropriate column.

When these have been sorted hold a plenary session in which each pair displays their sets and tells the class why they have sorted them the way they have. In other words identifying the characteristics of each set.

Teaching tip

In the extension activity on using random sets, remember there may be several ways of sorting them. Once the children have identified the characteristics, ask them if they could sort them in a different way.

At the beginning of the task, model the process and ask the children to help you. When they give suggestions, ask them why they chose to do it that way. Are they able to identify the characteristics they have used? For instance, 'That blue car goes with the red one because they have both got four wheels,' or 'The lorries go together because they all have more than four wheels.' This will encourage them to avoid random selections.

Move on to modelling a set that could be sorted by using more than one characteristic, such as both by colour and the number of wheels.

Encourage the children to articulate what characteristics are common in each set. Give each pair about 10 or 12 objects to sort.

Extension activities

❑ Provide each pair with a randomly picked set of objects and ask them to sort them. Follow this with a set of 3-D shapes/objects and ask them to sort them. Discuss with them the characteristics they had identified and used to sort them.

❑ Play the 'Odd one out' game. Give the children a set of shapes that can be sorted into two groups but where one shape will be the odd one out. Can the group identify it and say why it is the odd one out? (For example, one triangle, three squares and three rectangles.) Once they have understood the game move on to more complex sets which could be sorted by two characteristics. (For example, a blue circle, a blue square, a red square and a blue rectangle. In this case the odd one out could be either the red square because all the others are blue or the blue circle because all the others have four sides.)

❑ Ask the children to compile their own set of shapes and then challenge someone else to find the odd one out. You will need to be sure they are ready to do this and that they don't just pick a random set of shapes.

❑ As a homework task ask the children to collect pictures from magazines and newspapers to form a set. One of the pictures will be the odd one out. Challenge others to find it. For example, a child collects five pictures of land animals and one of a bird. These could then be displayed in the classroom or made into a scrapbook and left in the library for others to use. The answers could be under flaps or kept in the classroom. Some of the best could be included in the school newsletter for parents and families to try at home.

Assessment
- Discuss with each pair of children the characteristics of each set. Then with two pairs together, discuss the differences and similarities between their sets. (Compare and contrast.)

Sort the spellings

Information-processing skills: Sorting information

Key skills

- Communication
- Working with others

Subject links

- Literacy

Aim

- To identify the phonetic/spelling characteristics of words and sort them into sets.

Organisation

Pairs

Time

20 minutes

Resources

- Lists of words
- 'Sort tanks' thinking frame (page 131)

Outcomes

- The words will have been organised into sets with different spelling/phonetic characteristics and the children will be able to explain why each set is as it is.

Task

The children have to sort a collection of words into sets according to given criteria. Introduce the activity by modelling the process with the whole class. Write on the board a list of about ten words and tell the children you are all going to look for common characteristics that enable you to put the words into spelling sets. For example, all these words have a magic 'e' or these words have a silent letter in them. Generate a whole-class discussion and sort accordingly.

When everyone understands the task, organise the children into pairs and give each pair a list of 15 to 20 words. Ask them to identify the spelling characteristics of the words and sort them into sets. They can use the thinking frame on page 131 to record the words in each set.

When they have finished they can then show their sets to another pair and ask them to say what is the common characteristic of each set. Could they be sorted in a different way?

These sets could then be displayed with the characteristics of each set identified.

Teaching tip

You will need to select your lists of words carefully to match the abilities of each pair. Be prepared to accept sets that do not necessarily match your thinking. Remember the most important skill here is the thinking skill of sorting information, not just identifying the spelling/phonetic rule. Of course if the thinking is not consistent with the literacy knowledge of the children you will need to discuss this with the children and assist them in applying their knowledge more accurately.

The lists you provide can either use words or rules the children have already learned and act as a form of reinforcement, or be used to introduce new spelling rules.

Extension activities

❑ Give each pair a list of spelling rules and ask them to find words for each rule. Then the children write these out in a random way and give the list to another pair and ask them to sort them. When they have finished the two pairs discuss the thinking used to sort them.

❑ Give each pair a list of words and ask them to sort them into two groups according to a spelling rule. Ask them to write what the spelling rule is. (For example, plural rules for words that end in a consonant 'y' and vowel 'y', such as libraries and valleys.)

Name it

Task

Model the process of classifying by showing the children some signs or labels you might find in a supermarket, such as a sign that reads 'drinks' and another that reads 'vegetables'. Then ask them to suggest some items that you would find under each sign or on those particular shelves. Explain that all the items in the shop have been sorted into sets and each set has a special name. This is called 'classification'. Ask the children why they think shops do this.

Next, tell the children they are going to be given a set of photographs or pictures of different sorts of buildings. They have to look at each set and divide them into subsets. They then must be able to explain their reasoning and give each set an appropriate name. For example, 'All these buildings are used as homes', 'These buildings are shops' or 'These buildings are single storey.'

When each pair has sorted their pictures they could display them with their names for each set. They could use the thinking frame on page 132 to record their thinking. They then show these to the class and explain their reasoning. Or they could show their sets to another pair and ask them to think why they have sorted them in that way.

Teaching tip

You will need to collect a wide range of pictures of buildings. These could be from magazines or newspapers, or from commercially produced packs. The children could collect pictures themselves to use.

Remember the essential skill is the thinking skill of classifying, so encourage the children to explain their thinking when they name each set. If they have identified a common characteristic but used a name that is inappropriate, discuss this with them. You may want to then give them a more appropriate name to provide them with specific vocabulary.

Extension activities

❑ Use pictures of buildings from other countries or buildings from the past.

❑ Collect and cut out pictures of different types of household furniture (this could be a homework task) and ask the children to sort them and give each set a name, such as 'bedroom furniture' and 'kitchen furniture'.

❑ Give a group a collection of non-fiction books, such as animal books, books about people and art books, and ask them to sort them and name each set. This would serve as a practical way to introduce the classifications used in the school library.

❑ To follow up the introduction about shop labels why not take a group to the local supermarket? Give each group a list of items and ask them to find them in the shop and record the classification label they found them under.

Assessment

• Is the name of each set appropriate and can the children explain their reasoning?

What's on the box?

Task

Introduce the task to the class by showing them a television schedule for one day. Ask them to find two programmes that are of the same sort, such as dramas. When they have made some suggestions, ask them to explain why they have paired the two programmes together.

At this stage you should encourage the correct use of vocabulary for each category and generate a discussion about the common characteristics of each category.

Divide the class into pairs and give each pair a copy of a day's television programmes schedule. Each pair should then scan this schedule and identify the different types of programme. They should put these into sets and name each set. They should be able to identify between three and six categories. They could also try to identify any particular group of viewers that the programmes are aimed at.

Alternatively give each group a day's television schedule, ensuring that each group has a separate day so that a whole week's television programming is covered. Once each group has sorted and classified their day's programmes collate these and ask the children if there is a balance between the categories over the whole week. How do they know? Is it by the number of programmes in each category or by the total time these programmes take up in the schedule? (There is plenty of opportunity here to apply maths skills.)

Teaching tip

For younger Key Stage 2 children limit the schedule to the evening rather than the whole day.

For children with special educational needs you will need to simplify the schedule and lay it out in a more accessible way.

Support the thinking by providing a recording sheet with the classifications on and a definition for each one.

Classifying is an important scientific skill so when engaged in science activities relate that work to this so the children learn to apply the thinking skill of classifying to different areas of their learning.

Encourage the use of the correct vocabulary – 'classifying' and 'classification' rather than 'naming' and 'names'. Reinforce that classifications indicate a common set of characteristics or attributes.

Extension activities

❑ Once the categories have been identified the children could calculate the amount of time given to each category that day. Which is given the most viewing time?

❑ Another extension task is to design an evening's schedule that caters for the viewing habits of a family of two adults and three children using the categories already familiar to the children.

❑ Introduce the classification of animals in science by giving the children pictures of different animals in each classification and asking them to identify common characteristics of each set. For example, 'All these pictures are of birds', 'These animals have no legs' and 'These all have fur.' The children then have to give each set a classification name.

Assessment

- Discuss with the children their sets of programmes and the common characteristics of each set. Then ask them what each set/category is called. Are they using the correct vocabulary? (For example, documentary and drama.)

Getting dressed

Task

Whole-class activity

Show the class a shoe and a sock and ask the children where on the body they would wear them. Then ask them which one they would put on first. Then ask why the sock goes on first. Use this example to explain that when something has to be done in a series of steps it is important that each step follows on from the last to form a logical or 'sensible' order or sequence.

Next show the children a doll or teddy and some clothes for it. Ask the children to work out the logical sequence to dress it. Which piece of clothing goes on first? Which follows?

Individual task

Give the children the opportunity to dress a doll or teddy. When they have done so they then have to undress it and lay the clothes out in the order they are put on the doll or teddy.

When they have done this successfully and grasped the concept of a logical sequence give them photographs of different items of clothing or card cut-outs of clothes and ask them to lay them out in the sequence they would put them on if they were dressing themselves.

Plenary

Discuss with the children the sequences they have designed. Could the sequence be in a different order and still be logical?

Ask them to think of some other activities which have to be done in a logical sequence, such as cleaning their teeth or making a sandwich.

Teaching tip

Collect pictures from catalogues and magazines of different items of clothing to use for this activity.

You are trying to get the children to articulate their thinking process. Encourage language that illustrates sequencing and ordering. Focus on connective words and phrases, such as 'then', 'afterwards', 'following that' and 'once that is done'.

Introduce and encourage the use of the vocabulary associated with this thinking skill. Illustrate and use the words 'logical' and 'sequence' whenever possible.

When assessing the children it is important that you focus on the process through observation and questioning or discussion.

Extension activities

❏ Ask the children to write down some of the different activities that take place in school during a normal day. Ask them to write each one on a different piece of paper or card, then to give these to someone else and ask them to sequence them in order. The results can then be discussed by the children.

❏ Ask the children to recount the stages they go through when getting ready for bed. But to make it different ask them to think backwards from the time they are in bed to the time when they are told it's time for bed.

❏ Select five children whose birthdays are in different months. Tell them to stand up and hold a card in front of them with their birth month written on it. You could have a set of these ready and they pick the correct one. Then ask them to sort themselves into a sequence beginning with the birthday month nearest to January and finishing with the one nearest to December. The rest of the class could help or decide if they have the correct sequence.

❏ Write on the board a sequence involving several stages, such as making a slice of toast, but place one or more of the stages in the incorrect position in the sequence. Ask the children if they can spot the one in the wrong position. Can they explain why it is in the wrong position and where it should go?

Assessment

- Observe closely the process employed by the children to assess if it follows a logical sequence. Or ask the children to explain the process they used.

Stepping stones

Information-processing skills: Sequencing

Key skills

- ICT
- Communication
- Problem solving

Subject links

- ICT
- English

Aim

- To organise a sequence leading to the publication of a poem using a word-processor.

Organisation

Pairs

Time

1 hour

Resources

- Poetry books
- A computer
- 'Stepping stones' thinking frame (page 133)

Outcomes

- The children will have printed out a copy of a selected poem using a word-processor and identified the different stages in the process and recorded these in a flow diagram that serves as a set of instructions for others.

Task

Introduction

Ask the class what stepping stones are and where they might find them. Through discussion ensure they understand that the stones are points along a journey and they have to be used in the correct order or the journey can not be completed successfully without getting your feet wet!

Agree that any task has to be done in the correct sequence of steps if it is to be wholly successful. Ask the class for examples of such tasks. Reinforce with them the need to use the correct vocabulary of 'logical' and 'sequence'.

Working in pairs

Organise the children into pairs and explain that they have to select a poem they like from the selection of poetry books and copy and print it out using the word-processor. The end result must be attractive and appealing and can be to their own design. Although the printed outcome is important it is the process of identifying the logical order of actions that is most important. The children could record their thinking using the frame on page 133. So, as well as having the printed poem, they will also complete a flow diagram identifying the different stages or stepping stones needed to be followed in order to achieve this end result. This flow diagram could then be based on the stages identified in the thinking frame and used as a set of instructions to others on how to compose and print out text to any design.

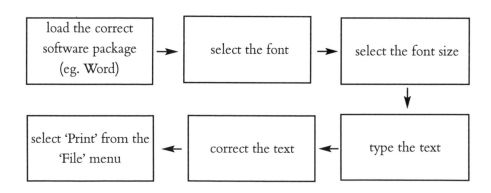

Teaching tip

Demonstrate and encourage the use of correct vocabulary whenever possible and discuss with the children the thinking processes used in determining the sequence. Ask them why certain actions are where they are and how they arrived at that decision.

For younger children or children with special needs you may want to produce a simple template with a predetermined number of action boxes. Start with a small number and gradually build up so the process is being broken down into smaller steps.

Extension activities

❏ The above task is a single linear flow diagram but some can contain alternative routes or stages. Discuss with the children examples of these. For example, making a cup of tea will be different for someone who takes sugar and someone who doesn't.

❏ Explain that at some points along the sequence it may be necessary to make an either/or decision which will lead to two separate routes or sequences.

❏ Ask them to create a flow diagram that demonstrates the sequence of events for children in the class who stop for dinner. They will need to consider the differences between those having sandwiches and those having a school dinner.

❏ Once they have completed their own design for the flow diagram introduce them to decision gates (either/or questions) and ask them to draw it out again including these gates.

Assessment

• You will be assessing the quality of the finished printed outcome (the poem), the flow diagram and the thinking identified on the thinking frame. The flow diagram must illustrate a logical sequence of actions and serve as a set of instructions for others to use.

**Information-
processing skills:
Comparing and
contrasting**

Key skills

- Communication
- Problem solving

Subject links

- Maths
- Art and design

Aim

- To compare and contrast two different objects and be able to identify some similarities and differences between the two.

Organisation

Whole class

Time

45 minutes

Resources

- Coats
- Teddies/dolls
- Books/toy cars

Outcome

- Children will have identified between three and six similarities and differences between two objects.

Same, similar or different?

Task

Show the class two identical objects, such as two dolls, teddies, books or items of clothing. Ask the children to tell you if they are the same. How do they know they are the same? What clues have they used to help them come to this conclusion? Explain that they are identifying features of the objects and checking to see if they are the same or different in some way.

Now show the class two similar but not identical coats (or two dolls or two toy cars). Ask them if they are the same or different in some way. What is the same about them? What is different about them? What is almost the same but not quite (similar)? What features have they looked at?

On the board write down the features or aspects of the objects they could use as indicators of how alike or unalike they are, such as the texture, size, colour, shape and number of arms.

Then ask them to say if each of the features is the same, different or similar. When they are confident in this process explain that they have been comparing and contrasting and that all information can be compared and contrasted.

Teaching tip

The key to this activity is the introduction of specific vocabulary. Start simply by using 'the same' and 'different', then move on to 'alike' and 'unalike' finishing with 'similar'.

Select your objects carefully ensuring that in the early stages the differences are very pronounced or obvious, then build up slowly and move towards more subtle differences between the objects.

Extension activities

❑ Ask pairs of children to pick two objects from the play area and write down three things that are similar and three things that are different.

❑ Extend this by giving them a set of three objects to compare and contrast.

❑ Explore the similarities and differences in the houses near to the school. What things are the same? (brick type/colour) What things are different? (front doors/colours)

Assessment

• Ask the children to write or draw the differences between two objects, then to identify the things that are the same and then the things that are similar. Are they able to identify these in labelled sets? Do they use the simplest vocabulary or are they using the more advanced language associated with the skill of comparing and contrasting?

Information-
processing skills:
Comparing and
contrasting

Key skills

- Communication
- Problem solving
- Working with others

Subject links

- Art and design

Aim

- To identify features of different pieces of art (or design objects) and compare and contrast those features.

Organisation

Groups of three

Time

45 minutes

Resources

- Copies of paintings
- Pieces of sculpture
- A collection of designed objects, such as watches, pens and rucksacks

Outcome

- Each group will have identified at least three similarities and differences between two pieces of art or designed objects.

Alike and unalike

Task

Show the class two portraits or paintings and ask them what they have in common. Then ask them what is different about them. Now show them two examples of a designed object, for example two different trainers. Ask the class in what way they are alike and in what way they are unalike.

Now give each group a set of pictures or designed objects and ask them to find at least three similarities and three differences between them. They should record these and their explanation of how the identified features are similar or different.

At first the children may focus on general features so you should aim to introduce them to the features of colour, tone, texture, line and so on.

At the end of the session, ask the children to share their findings with the class, encouraging the use of the words 'comparing', 'contrasting', 'comparison' and 'contrast'. Encourage them to describe the thinking processes they used in their discussions.

Teaching tip

Set up a carousel of activities that each group can visit. Ensure the pictures or items are on the same theme to ensure there are sufficient similarities. The children will at first find identifying differences easier than similarities. Discuss with the groups their findings and the similarities they have identified. Take into account your SEN children through mixed ability groups. The focus should be on the thinking employed rather than on the skill of writing reports. Emphasise the correct vocabulary and model it in your discussions with the groups.

Extension activities

❑ Groups can collect their own set of pictures or design objects and identify five similarities and five differences and then challenge another group to see if they can find the same. The two groups then discuss each other's findings and look for matches and differences.

❑ The process of comparing and contrasting can be used across the curriculum. For instance looking at homes in two different geographical areas; or in science using the process when examining materials.

Assessment

• Assess that at least three similarities and differences have been identified and reasons for choices given.

Information-processing skills: Analysing relationships

Key skills

- Application of number
- Communication
- Working with others
- Problem solving

Subject links

- Maths

Aim

- To identify the connection between objects or numbers in a set.

Organisation

Pairs

Time

15 minutes

Resources

- Number cards
- Items of clothing
- Pictures of shapes or actual shapes
- 'Links' thinking frame (page 134).

Outcomes

- The children will be able to articulate the connection/relationship between items in a set.

Links

Task

Show the class two plastic circle shapes of different sizes. Ask the children what they are and if they are the same. Explain that although they are both circles they are not identical. They are linked because they are both circles and because they are both made from the same material.

Next show the class a plastic square shape and a plastic rectangle. Ask the children if they are the same and if there is a link between them. Explain that they are linked because they are both shapes (or both have four sides) and they are both made from the same material.

Next show the class two articles of clothing such as a pair of mittens and a pair of gloves. Ask the children what the connection is between them. Explain that they are both articles of clothing and that another connection is that they are both worn on the hands.

Divide the class into pairs and give each pair either two number cards or two objects, and the thinking frame on page 134. Ask them to identify the characteristics of each object or number in the set and then make the connection between them and record their ideas on the thinking tool template. For example, if they pick the number cards 4 and 8, they could find that they are both even numbers, that 4 is half of 8, that 8 is double 4 and that they are both in the two times table.

Once each pair has grasped the concept of relationships then increase the number of items in the set. For example, the number cards for 3, 9, 15 and 21. (They are all odd and in the three times table.)

When the children have completed the task, ask some of them to show the class their thinking tool templates and describe the connection between the items in the set.

Then ask the children when this sort of thinking could be used.

Teaching tip

This is a crucial central skill in processing information and building understanding, so the numbers or items must be carefully selected to match the abilities of the children. Build on the mathematical knowledge of the children, slowly and carefully, only adding more items to the set when you are sure that they have understood the concept of analysing relationships. This activity can also be used to introduce new mathematical concepts and areas of learning.

Avoid using the word 'related' at this stage and use 'link' or 'connection' instead. Encourage the children to identify the link or connection and the common characteristic(s), for example 'They are linked because they are both circles and both made from plastic.'

Discuss with the class the relationship between different curriculum activities taught recently. For instance the connection between their work in art when they painted a landscape and their work in geography when they looked at deserts.

The plenary is an important aspect of this activity as it enables the children to see how this skill can be transferred to different contexts.

Extension activities

❑ In pairs again, Partner A gives the connection between the items in a set and Partner B has to suggest appropriate items for the set. For example, Partner A says the connection between the two items in the set is that they are both between 20 and 30. Partner B may then suggest the two items in the set are 24 and 27. They then discuss whether B's suggestion is appropriate. Or, Partner A says the link between the two items is that you can sit on them. Partner B then might suggest a stool and a chair.

❑ As confidence and skill increase extend the number of items in each set.

Assessment

- Assess whether the child can relate two objects by describing the connection between them.

Information-processing skills: Analysing relationships

Key skills

- Application of number
- Working with others
- Problem solving

Subject links

- Maths
- English
- Science

Aim

- To identify the connection between random objects or numbers in a set.

Organisation

Groups of three

Time

20 minutes

Resources

- Number cards (maths)
- Objects/materials (science)
- 'Links' thinking frame (page 134)

Outcome

- Children will be able to articulate the connection(s) between random numbers or items in a set.

Pick a card, any card

Task

Divide the class into groups of three.

From a set of number cards pick two cards at random. Now challenge the class to think of three links between them in three minutes. Each group records their thinking using the thinking tool template on page 134.

After three minutes ask the groups to share their links with the class. It is important at this stage to focus on the thinking process employed rather than the actual outcome.

Repeat the task.

Now increase the set to three random numbers.

In the plenary session, lead a discussion on possible links between different curriculum activities covered recently, for example relating work in geography to work in science.

Teaching tip

Focus on the thinking skill rather than on the outcome to begin with.

Encourage the children to articulate their thinking (metacognition) and to identify any subject knowledge or skills that helped them in the task.

Extension activities

❏ Each group selects two or three random numbers from a set of number cards. They think of links between the numbers and then challenge another group to find the links in three minutes.

❏ The group then makes a simple display by displaying the random numbers and underneath recording the link under a pull up flap. These can then be displayed on a board and are used as challenges for other groups.

❏ Instead of using number cards use word cards. For instance, use key vocabulary from previous areas of learning to reinforce or assess understanding.

❏ Use sets of objects instead of number or word cards. For instance a set of different materials linked to science work.

Assessment

• Assess whether the children are able to find three links between two numbers in a set. Ask them to explain their thinking. It is the actual thinking process which is most important at first. Then when the children are using this skill assess whether the links made are logical and relevant. Have the children used their previous subject knowledge to make the connection?

The 'Because' game

Reasoning skills: Giving reasons for opinions and actions

Key skills

- Communication
- Problem solving

Subject links

- Maths
- English
- Science (AT1 – Investigation activities)

Aim

- To enable children to become familiar with the why/because relationship.

Organisation

Individual

Time

10 minutes

Resources

- Stacking cubes
- Shapes
- Nesting boxes/shapes
- Set of five circles increasing in size

Outcomes

- The children will have sorted a set of objects according to a given criterion and will be able to explain their actions using the word 'because' in their response.

Task

Introduce the idea of giving reasons for answers and opinions by asking the children a series of simple questions and encouraging them to give their reasons using the word 'because' in their answers. For example:

'Why do you think we wear more clothes in the winter?'

'Why is it safer to cross the road at a pedestrian crossing?'

'Why do we use umbrellas?'

Now explain that they are going to be asked to put some objects in order and that they will have to explain why they put them in that order. Emphasise that they will need to use the word 'because' in their answers.

Demonstrate this by showing the class a set of pictures of animals, or write the names of the animals on the board. Ask the children to put them in order of size, starting with the smallest and finishing with the largest (horse, cat, elephant, mouse, dog). Then ask them how they would explain why they put them in that order to a visitor to the class. One child might say, 'I put the elephant last because I know it is the largest land animal. I then looked to see which was the smallest. Because a mouse is smaller than a cat, dog or horse I put the mouse at the beginning.'

Now ask them if there is any other way to order them, for example the slowest to the fastest.

Give each child a set of cubes or nesting boxes or circles of different sizes and tell them the criteria for sorting them, such as from the smallest to the largest.

Discuss their actions with the children, asking 'Why have you placed that object there/next?' Encourage them to respond with the word 'because'.

Teaching tip

The concept of using 'why' in a question and using 'because' as an aid to reasoning is a key one in reasoning skills. We should be encouraging their use by children as much as possible. In this way we can steer children away from value judgements and responses such as 'Because I like it.'

It may be necessary to model an appropriate answer because many children will not be familiar with the why/because relationship. For example, 'I moved this next because it is bigger than the red one,' or 'I picked this one because it is bigger than that one but smaller than this.'

This activity requires the teacher to work directly with the child observing closely and teasing out from them their reasoning through careful questioning.

Select the criteria for the task carefully to match the subject knowledge of the children.

Extension activities

❑ Encourage the refining of the children's language by modelling responses that refer to two criteria. For example, 'I put that one there because it is smaller than that one but larger than that one.'

❑ Ask the children to think of between three and five 'why' questions about animals that they could ask their family. They should then write down the answers ensuring they use the word 'because' in their answers. Tell them that if their parents don't use the word 'because' they should explain why they are writing the word 'because' in the answer. This can be a homework task.

❑ Every week have a 'why' question and answer session. The children can ask you or the class their 'why' question and you, or the class, answer using 'because' in the response.

Assessment
- Assess whether the child is able to justify their actions by using the word 'because' in their responses.
- Assess if the reasons given are appropriate.

Because

Reasoning skills: Giving reasons for opinions and actions

Key skills
- Communication
- Problem solving

Subject links
- PSHE

Aims
- To explore the opinions of others and the reasons for those opinions.

Organisation
Groups of four

Time
15 minutes

Resources
- The 'Because' thinking frame (page 135)

Outcomes
- The children will be able to express an opinion and give at least one reason for that opinion.

Task

Tell the children that they are going to work in groups and will be given a scenario to consider. Then each member of the group is to consider their response/opinion and tell the group what it is.

Stress that each child must give at least one reason for that opinion. It is acceptable for the rest of the group to explore this reasoning further if they feel it is inappropriate, ie a value judgement.

Examples of scenarios could include:

1. Tell the group that they are going to visit the fairground and have £5 to spend there. Give them a list of rides and stalls and the cost of each one. Each child has to tell the group how they would spend their money and the order in which they would visit the rides/stalls.

2. An uncle unexpectedly sends them £10. They have to decide which shop they will spend the money in and give their reasons. Give the group a list of shops to choose from, for example a toyshop, art shop, sports shop and computer shop.

3. If you were able to spend a special day doing anything you wanted, what would you do and where would you go?

4. If you could be anyone famous who would you be?

5. If you could be anyone from the past who would you be?

Each group should record the reasons for their opinions using the thinking frame on page 135.

Teaching tip

It is important that a culture of respect for each other's opinions is established. The purpose is not for children to criticise each other's opinions but for them to be able to articulate their thinking behind their opinions.

Encourage the children to avoid making value judgements such as, 'Because I like it,' or 'I just do.' By careful and sensitive probing it should be possible for children to respond by saying, 'I like it because…'.

Extension activities

❏ Play the 'Why?' game. The children work in pairs and ask each other for their opinion on a topic and one reason for that opinion. Child A asks Child B 'Why?' in response to Child B's answer. Child B gives their reason. Child A asks 'Why?' again and so on. Child A asks the question 'Why?' five times. The purpose of this activity is to get Child B to refine their answers and demonstrate their thinking.

❏ Encourage children to ask a range of questions using the words 'Who?', 'Why?', 'When?', 'How?' and 'Where?'. This can be done by making a set of key question cards with one of the above question words on each one. Another set of cards with topic areas, such as 'The Second World War', could be prepared. Child A picks one card from each set and has to use them in a question they formulate to Child B. For example, Child A picks the key question card with 'How?' on it and a topic card with ' The Second World War' written on it. He may then think of the question, 'How did the Second World War start?' Child B answers and Child A asks 'Why?' and so on.

Assessment

- The children can assess each other by recognising when an opinion is backed with an appropriate response. They could record each other's answers and the number of reasons given for each answer. This information can then be fed back to the individual child and the teacher.

The time capsule

Task

Tell the class that each group is going to be given a list of things found in a time capsule and that they have to deduce whose time capsule it is. Remind them that each item is a clue and will assist them in arriving at a deduction about whose time capsule it is. However, they should not assume the identity of the person from just one item. They will need to relate it to the other items, otherwise they might reach the wrong deduction. For instance, in the example below, a broomstick could lead them to think of Harry Potter but it may just as likely be associated with The Worst Witch. If the other items do not seem to be associated with their first deduction then it is likely that it is incorrect, and they will need to look for other connections between the items.

Give each group a list of five things found in the capsule. Tell them to record their thinking using the thinking frame on page 136. In the capsule are a pair of spectacles, a wand, a railway ticket, a drawing of a cupboard under the stairs and a picture of a broomstick. This time capsule belonged to Harry Potter.

Plenary: Each group tells the class the items in their capsule and whose they think it is. The rest of the class then question them about the significance of each item and how it led them to their conclusion.

Teaching tip

Explain to the children that this is not a guessing game but that they are going to be like detectives and use the clues to help solve the mystery. One clue on its own may not be enough so they will need to consider all the clues and the relationship between them.

Extension activities

❑ Each group can select a famous person, living or dead, and research that person. Once the research is completed they select five items to go into the capsule. They then give this list to another group and challenge them to deduce whose capsule it is.

❑ Instead of a time capsule it could be the contents of someone's suitcase returning from holiday abroad. Using the items the group has to deduce where that person had gone on holiday.

❑ Alternatively, the children could be given a book bag with items relevant to a specific book and they have to deduce which book it represents.

❑ Older children or children who demonstrate good deduction skills could be given one item at a time, starting with the hardest or most obscure. After they have been given each item they try to deduce whose capsule it is from. They are given five points if they deduce correctly after the first clue, four after the second and so on. Many children will guess at first and then begin to use deducing skills and this activity is a good way of demonstrating the difference between a guess, an educated guess and full deduction.

Assessment

- Assess whether the group has deduced the correct person.

- Assess whether the group has made wild guesses or used the items to lead them to the correct answer. Examine the thinking tool to do this. It may also be helpful to discuss with them their thinking.

Leaping from stone to stone

Reasoning skills: Explaining thinking

Key skills

- Communication
- Problem solving
- Application of number

Subject links

- Maths
- All subjects

Aims

- To enable children to break down their thinking into steps and explain how they got from one step to another.

Organisation

Individual

Time

10–15 minutes

Resources

- The 'Stepping stones – 2' thinking frame (page 137)

Outcomes

- The children will have recorded each step of their thinking and articulated how they moved from one stepping stone to the next.

Task

Challenge the children to start at a given number and finish at another given number in a given number of steps. For example:

Start at 60 and finish at 7 using four steps.

The child might go from 60 to 50 to 30 to 15 to 7.

They record these figures on the stepping stones on the thinking frame on page 137, but also crucially explain how they got from one number to the next. So, for instance, they might write, 'I subtracted 10 which took me to 50. Then I took away another 20 which took me to 30. Next I halved 30 which took me to 15, and finally I subtracted 8 which took me to the final number 7.'

Clearly the teacher will select appropriate numbers for the ability of the children doing the task.

You could present older children with a scenario involving the exchange of money in a shop. For example, you are the shopkeeper and someone buys an item that costs £3.32. He gives you a £10 note. Work out how much change to give him. Using the thinking frame on page 137, the children can record the steps and the thinking between them. For instance:

£3.32 ➡ £3.40 ➡ £3.50 ➡ £4.00 ➡ £10.00

NOTE: This thinking frame can also support thinking in other subjects. For instance, in design the children can record the stages in the development of a project. They then explain how they moved on from each stage, and why they proceeded in that way. So they might record that they added a crosspiece to a wooden frame because they noticed that the frame was twisting slightly when pressure was put on it. Or that they had added some coloured wool to a mask because it hid the jagged edges.

Teaching tip

Explaining one's thinking is a core thinking skill (metacognition) and it is through being able to do this that understanding and effective learning come. Remember Alison? She was the girl who said, 'Thinking is like a journey from one idea to the next.' (Page 4) Well, all journeys involve a number of steps. It is these steps, or movement from one stepping stone to another, that demonstrate the thinking process. The stones act as markers or actual ideas along the way.

Explaining one's thinking in maths is a core skill and this activity will help to reinforce that process and can also act as an assessment tool to assess the level of mathematical knowledge and skill being applied.

The thinking tool can be used in any activity which requires children to explain their thinking.

Extension activities

❏ Instead of giving the children the number of steps they are to use they can use as many, or as few, steps as they want to solve a problem. For example:

> Take 537 away from 1000.

The child then records their thinking on the thinking tool. So, for instance they might record:

> 537 add 3 is 540.
> 540 is 60 away from 600.
> 600 add 400 is 1000.
> So, 400 add 60 add 3 is 463.

Assessment

• Assess not only if the steps are logical and correct but the thinking that was used in moving from one step to another.

Decisions, decisions!

Task

Tell the class that they are going to have to make a decision about something but that they must come to this decision after they have considered a range of evidence and used their reasoning skills. Emphasise that they are not going to make this decision based on guesswork or their own feelings towards the situation.

Think of the problem or context and pose the problem to the class. For example:

❑ 'Should we go out to play today?'
❑ 'Where would be a good place to visit for the day?'
❑ 'What should we put on the display board?'
❑ 'How could we rearrange the classroom?'

Tell the children to use the evidence available to them before they arrive at their decision. They may need to consider the weather conditions, the behaviour of the class, whether work has been finished and so on.

Encourage them to explain their reasoning as well as their decision. Ask them what evidence they took into account before reaching this decision.

Teaching tip

In many ways this is the culmination of a range of thinking skills. The ability to make an independent judgement calls upon increasingly sophisticated thinking strategies.

Start with the immediate and within one's own school context. Encourage children to think about the sorts of evidence that would be useful to consider before making their decision.

This skill can be used in many plenary sessions.

Extension activities

❑ Pose the challenge 'Which is the most popular food at lunch-time?' The children will have to collect evidence before they can arrive at their decision. This may involve data gathering by visiting different classes and collecting evidence, or asking the school dinner supervisors or kitchen staff.

❑ In science ask the children which is the most common material used for clothing.

❑ In geography which of these three places do they think is the most popular destination for a family holiday? Florida, Scotland or Australia?

❑ In design technology which of these sorts of footwear would be best for a walk in the hills? Sandals, trainers, wellington boots or leather shoes?

Assessment
• Assess whether the decision is clear and the evidence and reasoning have been articulated clearly.

Making reasoned decisions

Task

Tell the children that they are going to be posed a problem and that they have to make a decision about it. Explain that this decision must be a value judgement but one based on careful consideration of a range of evidence that they will have to collect.

Ask them what they think is the most popular television programme for children of their age (or another specified age range).

Now tell them that they have 10 minutes to think about the evidence they will need to collect before they make their decision and how they will go about collecting this evidence.

Then give them about half an hour to collect this evidence. This may involve going to other classes so make sure you arrange this with other teachers first.

Once the evidence has been collected the children are given about 10 minutes to arrive at their decision.

Ask each group to give their decision and to say what evidence they collected. Let the rest of the class question them about their decision and the evidence that was collected.

Teaching tips

Encourage the transfer of this skill into everyday situations where decisions have to be made.

It is acceptable to change decisions if new or conflicting evidence becomes apparent.

Reinforce the fact that you do not want them to make value judgements but to carefully consider the implications of evidence before arriving at their decision. Also explain that you want them to come to a consensus within the group, so it may be necessary to persuade someone within the group that the group decision is a reasonable one based on the evidence. This will be most successfully achieved if there is a culture of open but sensitive debate within the class.

Extension activities

❏ Ask the children which they think is the most common bird to visit the school grounds. Ask them to consider the evidence they will need and how they will go about collecting this evidence. This skill is a core one in science when thinking about designing an investigation (AT1).

❏ Once the children have grasped the concept and are becoming skilful you can pose a question and 'drip feed' them pieces of evidence. After each piece of evidence they make their decision. Does their decision change as new evidence is presented? Explain that this is acceptable and often the way we think. We can only come to a decision based on the evidence available at the time, and it is perfectly acceptable to change one's decision as long as it is based on the careful consideration of new evidence. For example, ask the class to decide whether January (or any month about to begin) will be a wet month. Now collect daily weather records and at the end of each day ask them for their decision. This of course may change daily. It is only after all the daily records have been considered and compared to data for the other months of the year that a judgement can be made on the basis of all the evidence.

Assessment

- Have the children arrived at a decision? Is the decision reasonable in relation to the evidence collected? Are they able to explain how they used this evidence? (What did they learn from it?)

What, when, how?

**Enquiry skills:
Asking relevant
questions**

Key skills

- Communication
- Working with others

Subject links

- Science
- History
- Geography

Aims

- To know the difference between relevant and irrelevant questions and information.
- To discover relevant information through careful questioning.

Organisation

Pairs

Time

30 minutes

Resources

- A guest to the classroom

Outcomes

- The children will have discovered specific information through asking relevant questions.
- The children will be able to sort questions into relevant and irrelevant questions.

Task

Invite a guest (or a group of guests) into the class so that the children can discover what they do and the sort of person they are. They can only do this through asking relevant questions.

They have to find out:
- ❑ one thing about the guest's family
- ❑ three things about the guest's occupation
- ❑ one thing about his/her interests/hobbies

The children should work in pairs. They can only ask the guest five questions. When they have finished asking their questions they must record the things they have discovered.

When everyone has had the opportunity to question the guest(s) ask the class to share with everyone all the things they have discovered. Record this information on the board.

	Relevant information	Irrelevant information
Family		
Occupation		
Interests		

At the end of the questioning section ask the children to tell the class the facts/information they have discovered. Then ask the children to sort these into relevant and irrelevant information. To do this they will need to refer back to the objective of the task.

Discuss with the class what questions gained irrelevant information and how these could have been improved. Ask the guest to say which sort of questions were most useful in enabling them to give relevant information.

Teaching tip

Create opportunities for children to learn information for themselves through the skill of asking relevant questions, that is for the children to recognise that relevant questions gain relevant information and irrelevant questions gain irrelevant information. This skill is best learned through a group or paired activity where the less confident can be supported by others. Even if a child is finding it difficult to formulate their own questions they can learn through listening to the questions posed by others, and through the analysis of the types of questions asked.

By setting a limit on the number of questions that can be asked, you make children think more carefully about the question they want to ask before posing it.

Extension activities

❑ Ask the children to work in groups of four to discover what the troll had for lunch. One child plays the part of the troll, and the others the Billy Goats Gruff. The troll thinks of something he might have had for his/her lunch, or the teacher writes some suggestions down on cards and the troll picks one of these cards. The three goats have a total of ten questions in which to discover what the troll had for lunch. If they discover this within ten questions they can cross the bridge.

❑ With older children, discuss how asking too specific questions at the start is a waste of questions. It is better to ask general questions that eliminate large areas of irrelevant possibilities. For example, 'Did you have chips?' is too specific. A better question might be 'Did you eat a hot or cold meal?'

❑ Ask the older children to work in pairs to think of five things they would like to discover about each other. They should write down their five questions or they could have a scribe. They then give each other their questions and write their answers to the questions given to them. Did everyone find out what they wanted to know? Were the questions relevant and could they improve them?

Note: ensure that the children understand not to ask personal questions that could offend or are not appropriate. Discuss what would be appropriate and what would not be appropriate.

Assessment

- By determining the amount of relevant information learned by the questioner(s) you will be able to determine the relevancy of the questions. How much was learned within the set number of questions?

- Can the children distinguish between relevant and irrelevant information and relevant and irrelevant questions? Are they able to reword a question so that it becomes more relevant?

- Are they able to apply this skill to other curriculum activities? For instance, asking relevant questions in history to find out more about the subject being studied; or in geography to discover facts about their local area.

Enquiry skills: Asking relevant questions

Key skills

- Communication
- Working with others

Subject links

Pupils will apply the skills of enquiry in most subjects, but in this particular case there are close links to:

- English – speaking and listening
- Science – classification of animals

Aims

- To know the difference between relevant and irrelevant questions and identify examples of both.
- To know the difference between open and closed questions.
- To ask relevant questions to discover relevant information.

Organisation

Groups of four

Time

45–60 minutes

Resources

- Tape recorder (optional)

Outcomes

- The children will have asked a series of questions that enable them to identify a mystery animal.
- The children will be able to identify which questions they asked were relevant and which were irrelevant.
- The children will be able to distinguish between an open and a closed question.

Twenty questions

Task

Working in groups of four, one child thinks of an animal and the other three have 20 questions to discover which animal it is. They should keep a record of the number of questions asked, or record the activity on a tape recorder.

When the groups have completed the activity ask the class to share with everyone all the things they have discovered. The purpose of this is to enable the children to start to be aware of the different sorts of questions that could be asked. For example, closed questions receive very narrow and specific answers; open questions receive more general and wider answers.

Try to draw out the point that at the beginning of the questioning they need to be asking questions that eliminate large classifications of animals, such as 'Do you have fur?'

Also ask the children if they wasted any questions, and why they were a waste. In what way were they irrelevant? If you have recorded the activity the group could listen to the recording and analyse their own questions.

Now go on to repeat the activity so that the other three members of the group have a turn thinking of an animal and the others ask the questions. Who asked the least number of questions?

Teaching tip

Start the activity by telling the class they will be playing a game, always a guarantee of getting their attention and interest! Explain the purpose of the activity and the rules, and divide the class into groups of four. It is recommended that these be mixed ability to give confidence and support to the less able.

Play the game once and then draw the class together to discuss the process and the questions asked. The purpose of this is to enable them to ask more focused questions when they play it again.

If possible, let the children record the activity so that they can analyse the questions they asked.

Repeat the activity so that all members of the group have the opportunity to think of an animal.

Extension activities

❑ Instead of asking the children to choose an animal they could choose to be a figure from history or a place in the world.

❑ With the whole class, simulate a press conference. Two or three children play the roles of survivors of a shipwreck (they will need to be briefed in advance), or you could ask the headteacher, other staff or parents. The rest of the class act the role of journalists who have to question the survivors to discover the full story of the shipwreck. At this point they have no information so they must discover everything through their questioning. When they have discovered all or most of the key information, which they record in note form as the press conference proceeds, ask the survivors to give the class feedback on the experience of being questioned. Were there any irrelevant questions? Were the questions closed or open? Were there any probing questions? Afterwards the journalists could work in pairs to write the first page of a newspaper giving the full story.

Assessment

- Assess the children through listening to the questions they ask. Keep a tally of the number of relevant questions they ask compared to the irrelevant questions asked. Do they ask more relevant than irrelevant questions?

- Do the children move from 'guessing' to focused questions? Do they display independent thinking and/or collaborative thinking?

Problems, problems, problems!

Task

Give the class the following scenarios and ask them to think about possible problems they might encounter and have to overcome.

❑ A family of two parents and three children decide to get a pet. They have never owned a pet before. What questions do they need to ask themselves? For example:

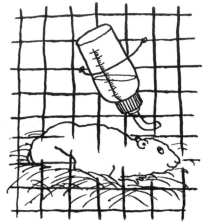

'What sort of pet should we get?'
'Where will we keep it?'
'What will it cost to keep it?'
'Who will look after it?'

❑ When the children get up one day and look outside it is snowing. What questions do they need to ask themselves, or their parents? For example:

'What shall I wear?'
'How cold is it?'
'How will I get to school?'

❑ Tell the children to imagine they are living in the desert and have to build a home. What questions do they need to ask themselves when thinking about the sort of home they have to build?

❑ Repeat this activity but this time the scenario is a cold land.

Teaching tip

As we all know, life can be full of problems, many of which are posed by factors outside our direct control. For example, when the mortgage rate goes up, we have to think of ways of meeting the extra expense.

Some problems become more difficult to solve because of a lack of anticipation or awareness of current factors. This particular thinking skill requires children to anticipate and identify the problems themselves.

Your role in this activity is to guide the discussion that arises from each scenario. You will need to use careful questioning to direct and focus their thinking. Initially the discussion will be in the form of a 'brainstorm', in which you value all contributions. Then you will evaluate the responses, identifying patterns or groups of ideas. Each response will enable you to focus the thinking of the children. Then it is up to you whether you then extend the activity and ask the children to find solutions to subsequent problems.

Extension activities

❑ There are obvious links here to design and technology tasks. Give the children a design brief and ask them to define the problems they might have to overcome. As the project continues they should be encouraged to identify any problems that have arisen. There are clear opportunities here to refer to the thinking skills of evaluation. For instance, a design brief might be to design a set of clothes to wear when playing in the snow.

❑ Look for opportunities to link this skill to other areas of work. For instance, when studying history can the children identify the problems their great grandparents would face if they were brought back to life today?

❑ In geography, what problems might have to be overcome by someone wanting to travel around the world?

Assessment

- Are the children able to identify possible problems arising from specific situations?
- Are the children able to sort these into categories?
- Do the children know that a problem is a difficulty that has to be overcome?

Your assessment will come through observation of their responses. The essential element is whether they can pose problems of their own arising from their everyday experiences.

Enquiry skills: Posing and defining problems

Key skills

- Communication
- Working with others
- Problem solving

Subject links

- Design and technology
- PSHE

Aims

- To define and pose problems within a given scenario.
- To sort problems into categories.

Organisation

Groups of four to six

Time

30–45 minutes

Resources

- Paper
- Black/whiteboard

Outcomes

- The children will have identified a set of problems that have to be overcome within the given scenario.
- The children will have categorised these problems into different areas.

Wheelchair

Task

Tell the children that a new child who is wheelchair-bound is to start school. Ask them to define the problems that may be encountered by the new child in your school.

Begin with a 'brainstorm' in small groups and then bring together all the ideas from the groups. Write them on the board.

Then ask if it is possible to group these ideas together into clusters so that each becomes a different problem area that has to be overcome. For example:

❏ access to different areas of the school
❏ access to areas of the curriculum
❏ play times
❏ outside visits

Each group could sort these and then report their ideas back to the class. Is there common agreement? Do they think these problems are insurmountable? What do they think is the most difficult problem to overcome? Which are the easiest to overcome?

Teaching tip

You will need to be sensitive about how you deal with the issue of disability. Ensure that all the children understand the nature of the disability, and that they understand what it means in real terms to be wheelchair-bound. It would be good if you could provide a wheelchair for the children to experience.

You will need to facilitate a 'brainstorm' through valuing everyone's contribution whether it is relevant or not. Later you can help the children to eliminate irrelevant ideas through careful questioning. Help the children to look for connections between the given ideas to assist in the process of putting them into categories.

When the 'brainstorm' is over, direct the groups to define at least two problems to overcome in each category. Allow 15 to 20 minutes for this section of the activity. Then ask the groups to report back to the rest of the class. This could be done by each group producing an A1 size display to pin around the room, and for the group to explain their ideas to the class.

Extension activities

❏ It is to be expected that the children would want to complete the activity by seeking solutions to these problems. Each group could take responsibility for thinking about one specific area identified in your class discussion and produce a display defining the problems and possible solutions. These could then be compiled into a report and presented to the school governing body.

❏ There are many opportunities for applying this thinking skill in other areas of the curriculum. In design and technology any design brief requires the designer to identify problems that will have to be overcome. For example, designing a vehicle that can carry an egg over different terrain, and in history defining the problems that had to be overcome when storming a castle.

❏ Posing problems for others to solve can be an activity that generates a lot of fun for children. For example, working in pairs, one of the children has to pose three problems that have to be overcome when starting a new school. The other child has to give possible ways of overcoming the three problems posed.

❏ In pairs, one of the children thinks of an animal and tells their partner that they will wake up the next day as that animal. Can they pose three problems that they might have to overcome as that animal?

Assessment

• Each group will have produced a set of defined problems that can be assessed for relevance to the objective. How relevant are they? Are they able to define what a problem is? Can they apply this thinking skill in other situations?

Enquiry skills:
Planning what to do

Enquiry skills: Planning what to do

Key skills

- Communication
- Working with others

Subject links

- Geography
- Art
- Religious education

Aims

- To enable the children to know that planning ahead is an essential part of enquiry.
- To practise planning for given tasks.
- To know that planning focuses thinking and makes carrying out the task more effective.

Organisation

Whole-class activity

Time

30 minutes

Resources

- Black/whiteboard
- Paper and pens

Outcome

- The children will have identified what has to be discovered and how this will be done.

Making plans

Task

Tell the children that they have to find out about their local area or a particular place, like the local church or mosque. They are to plan what they want to find out and how they are going to do this.

Begin with a 'brainstorm' by asking them what they would like to find out. List these ideas as questions on the board. For example, they might want to find out the age of the church/mosque. This could be written as the question 'How old is the building?'

Then tell the children they are going to have to plan how they will find out what they want to discover.

Write the question they want answering on the board and then ask the children how they will find the answer.

❑ Could they ask someone, and if so who?
❑ Would a visit to the church help, and if so how?
❑ Could they use a book, and if so where might they find it?
❑ Could they use any other source of information, like the Internet?

Next to each question write their ideas for what they need to do and how they will do this.

Now set them off on their own research about the local area. Ask them to write out their questions and their plan.

82

Teaching tip

Choose situations that are familiar to the children and within their own experience. Explain that planning means thinking ahead and determining what needs to be done and how it will be done.

Use simple examples, such as if they have to get up very early the next day to go on holiday or go out for the day, what will they need to do the night before to ensure this happens?

Extension activities

❑ For older children you could lead a discussion, or ask them in pairs, to put the things that need to be done in order.

❑ In art the children could be set the task of planning and making a puppet in pairs or small groups. Ask them to plan what they will need to do before they start, when they are making the puppet and after they have made it.

❑ Use the opportunity to ask the children to plan what to do whenever you set them a task. This enables them to acquire the correct disposition when actively engaged in their own learning.

Assessment

As this is a whole-class activity your assessment will be by observation.

- Assess whether the children are able to plan ahead by stating simply what they want to discover and how they will achieve this. At first they will probably only be able to give one way for each. As they progress they should be able to give at least two ways for each.

A day out

Task

Tell the children that they are going to plan a class day trip.

You can set the place to visit linked to your current work, or ask the children where would be a suitable place to visit.

Ask the children to work in groups and think about what needs to be done when planning the trip. What sources of information will they use? What will they do with the information?

Bring the groups together for a whole-class discussion.

Can they sort their ideas into different aspects of the trip? This could be done by thinking about what needs to be done now, nearer to the trip and immediately before the trip. This gives a structure to the thinking.

Now each group has to take responsibility for planning a specific aspect of the preparation for the trip, such as the travel arrangements, booking admission, costings and a letter to parents.

When they have completed their section of the plan they have to report back to the class explaining what needs to be done and what sources they used to find out.

Teaching tip

You will need to be prepared to allow the children the freedom to use a wide range of sources of information, such as the telephone, fax machine, the Internet and timetables. This will probably mean that you will need to arrange supervision by a classroom assistant or parent.

You will need to observe each group as they proceed and give guidance if necessary. You will have to use your professional judgement as to how long you will allow them to proceed down 'blind alleys'. But remember that an essential part of learning is to learn from failures by identifying what went wrong and how these mistakes can be rectified.

Extension activities

❏ If you want more of a challenge ask the children to plan a trip to Euro Disney, but make it clear this is a hypothetical trip or you might have a riot if at the end you tell them they are not really going!

❏ Again in groups set other shared tasks. For instance:
- organising a picnic
- making a display
- giving a presentation to the class

Each group has to:
- plan what to do
- establish what has to be done
- decide who is going to do it
- decide when it has to be done by
- decide how they will know if they have been successful

Assessment

• Assess the quality of the plan. Does it fulfil the set objective? Does it define clearly what has to be done and how it will be achieved?

Enquiry skills: How to research

Key skills
- Communication
- ICT

Subject links
- Geography
- Design and technology

Aims
- To enable children to formulate questions and to seek answers from a source.

Organisation
Individual or pairs

Time
Open-ended

Resources
- ICT and non-fiction texts

Outcomes
- The children will have found information relevant to a given task statement.
- The children will have formulated questions and found the answers.

Search it out

Task

Organise the children into pairs or let them work as individuals. Give each individual or pair one of the following tasks:

❑ Find out about the work of the fire brigade.
❑ Discover as much as you can about transport at sea.
❑ Learn about how clothes are made.

These are deliberately broad in their nature. At first one could expect the children to 'dive into' a range of sources provided and produce a varied set of unconnected facts. This method, of course, is unstructured and almost random in its approach. What we are aiming for is to give the process of research some structure and focus.

Encourage the children to think about the question(s) they could ask about the 'subject' to be researched.

Encourage them to appraise the source material. Is it likely to provide relevant information? Whereabouts in the source are they likely to find what they are looking for? Do they know what they are looking for? Are there other sources they could use?

Incorporate English/literacy skills in reading for information.

Tell the children to write a question relevant to the task statement, then to research and find the answer and to identify the source of information.

Task	My question	What I found out	Where I found my information

Teaching tip

At this stage in a child's development they are dependent on the teacher for clear guidance on how to research. This entails the following:

❑ Sources to be used in research are provided by the teacher.

❑ The more able learners can select a resource but are unable to judge whether it is suitable.

❑ The teacher sets the task.

❑ The more able learners can change the task statement into an appropriate question (see the 'Asking relevant questions' skill activity on page 74).

The children will work through these two levels of ability:

Level 1: The teacher sets the task and provides sources for the children to use to complete the task.

Level 2: The teacher sets the task and the children formulate a question to be answered through using a source selected by them.

There are many sources available including books, magazines, newspapers, television, radio and ICT.

The role of the teacher is to guide the children through the activity ensuring they are applying the skills learned through their work in English/literacy. Or the teacher may wish to teach these skills through this activity. If this is the case, ensure that the focus on the thinking skill is not lost, by emphasising it at the beginning of the lesson and referring back to it during the course of the lesson. The duration of this activity is deliberately open-ended to allow for different school circumstances, such as the size of the class and the availability and amount of source material.

Extension activities

❑ There will be many opportunities to develop this skill within your own schemes of work and during literacy lessons.

❑ As the children become more confident and skilled, extend the activity by asking them to increase the number of questions they are to research. Also increase the number of sources they can use in their research. Vary the types of sources to include a range of texts and ICT.

❑ If possible arrange for an 'expert' to visit the class so that children can ask them questions they have formulated. For instance a fire-fighter or dressmaker could visit the class and the children could question them either before they carry out their reading task or after to extend and validate the information they have discovered.

Assessment

• Assess which level the children are working at and whether the answers they have found are relevant.

The children will be working at either level 1 or 2 (see Teaching tip).

More able Year 2 children may be working at level 3 (see activity for Key Stage 2).

Enquiry skills: Researching

Key skills

- Communication
- ICT

Subject links

- PSHE

Aims

- To enable learners to formulate relevant questions to set tasks.
- To enable learners to use a variety of source materials and to judge their appropriateness.
- To enable learners to make a decision based upon their research.

Organisation

Individual

Time

Open-ended

Resources

- Wide variety including ICT

Outcomes

- Children will have used research skills to come to a decision about which career they would like to pursue.

When I grow up I want to be...

Task

Tell the children that each of them has to choose a future career from the following list (or choose their own):

- ❏ Doctor
- ❏ Pilot
- ❏ Fashion designer
- ❏ RSPCA officer
- ❏ Teacher
- ❏ Mechanic
- ❏ Farmer

They should select three from the list that initially attract them. Then they should research each of these three by formulating a set of questions they want to find the answers to, and list the things that they have discovered from their research that attracts them to the job.

Finally they have to select just one and give their reasons for their choice.

When they have completed the task each child has to report back to the class giving their selection, reasons, sources used and an evaluation of the source and the key questions they asked at the beginning of the task.

They could use a thinking tool like the one below to record work.

	Job	Job	Job
Key questions			
What I found out and sources			
What I like about the job			
Reasons for choices			

THINKING SKILLS

Teaching tip

The aim of this activity is to move the learner from dependence on the teacher to independence. Levels 1 and 2 are covered in the Key Stage 1 activity.

Level 3: The teacher sets the task and the learner formulates appropriate questions for one source selected by the learner, and is able to judge the appropriateness of the source but with adult help.

Level 4: The learner can formulate questions on a theme and select and use a variety of sources. He or she is able to judge the appropriateness of the sources but with adult help.

Level 5: The learner can formulate correctly framed questions for any resource. The learner can select a variety of sources and judge their appropriateness for him/herself.

The role of the teacher is to guide and support the children through the activity, moving them from dependence to independence. The teacher should be ensuring the children are using skills learned in literacy, or can teach these skills through this activity. However, it is essential that there is a focus on the thinking skill by emphasising it and referring to it during the course of the activity.

This is an open-ended activity to allow for different school circumstances.

Ensure there are adequate and varied resources available within school and that the children are aware that there are other sources they could access outside school. Use ICT (Internet) to provide as wide a range of sources as possible.

Extension activities

❑ Older or more able children could list not only the things that attract them to each job but also the things that they discovered that they did not like. This requires them to balance advantages against disadvantages in order to focus their thinking.

❑ There will be many opportunities for children to use this skill in your current work in other subjects. For instance:
- in geography to discover as much as possible about icebergs and glaciers
- in history to learn about the life of Queen Victoria

Assessment
- Assess which level the children are working at. They will be working at levels 3, 4 or 5 (see Teaching tip). Children with a special educational need may be working at levels 1 or 2 (see Key Stage 1 activity).

What happens next?

Task

Tell the children a story about seeing a lorry pass the house loaded with the following: bricks, window frames, doors, timber and slates. Ask them to predict the possible outcome if this lorry delivers the above to a house further down the street.

After the obvious reply that a house is being built try to draw out from them other possible outcomes, such as:

❏ A house is not being built but an extension to a house is being built.
❏ The owner of the house is a builder and needs the materials for his business.
❏ The driver lives at the house and is popping home for something.

Think of situations in which there are several possible outcomes. Put the children into small groups and encourage them to think of other outcomes besides the obvious ones. For instance, what are the possible outcomes of a netball match arranged between two schools?

❏ School A wins.
❏ School B wins.
❏ The match is drawn.
❏ School A can't come and the game is called off.
❏ School B can't come and the game is called off.
❏ It rains and the match is called off.

Now create the opportunity for the children to predict the outcome of their actions before they start an activity. For instance, provide them with a flowerpot, some compost, a packet of seeds and a watering-can and tell them they are going to grow some flowers/beans (or any suitable plant you choose). Tell them they are going to grow three flowers – one pot will be watered every day, one will be watered every four days and one won't be watered at all.

Ask the children to predict the outcome for each flower.

Let the children plant the seeds and water their three pots according to the plan above. After a week ask them to say if their predictions appear to be coming true. Repeat every week. At the end ask them to state which predictions were fulfilled.

Teaching tip

At the start when teaching children the skill of predicting outcomes ask the question 'What do you think will happen?' Then explain that when they say what they think might happen they are making a 'prediction' and that what happens is the 'outcome'. When you are sure they are comfortable using these expressions, use them when discussing the activities with them, and encourage the children to use them.

Use the opening two activities opposite to explain that there may be more than one possible outcome. Judging which are the most likely is dealt with in the Key Stage 2 activity for this skill.

The investigations into growing flowers and washing material (see Extension activities) are not intended to be fair scientific tests but situations which neatly provide the opportunity for the children to practise making predictions. If you want them to be fair tests then you will need to provide adult supervision while the children plant the seeds, water the pots, dirty the cloth and wash the cloth.

Extension activities

❑ Ask the children to dirty three pieces of the same cotton material. You could use paint or dirt. Then tell them they are going to wash each piece in a different way to see which method cleans the cloths best. Ask them to predict which one will be the cleanest.

Wash the first one in washing powder/liquid, the second with a bar of soap and the third in plain water.

Compare the results with their predictions.

Assessment

- Assess the level of relevancy of the children's predictions. Do they make wild guesses or do they base their predictions on knowledge or their own experiences?

- Do the children use the correct vocabulary?

Enquiry skills: Predicting outcomes

Key skills

- Communication
- Working with others

Subject links

- PSHE
- Science

Aims

- To make predictions about possible outcomes and to judge which are the most likely.
- To compare outcomes to predictions made.

Organisation

Pairs or small groups

Time

30–40 minutes

Resources

- Paper

Outcomes

- The children will have an ordered list of possible outcomes.

Crystal ball gazing

Task

Create opportunities for the children to make predictions about the possible outcomes of an activity. For example:

1. What are the possible outcomes of a teenager starting to smoke?

   It is likely, at first, that the children will say that he or she will die of lung cancer. Point out to them that this is not the only possible outcome. Ask them in pairs or small groups to list all the possible outcomes they can think of in ten minutes.

   Discuss with the class their ideas and list them on the board. (Do not make judgements about them at this stage.) Then ask them to list them in order of likelihood from the most likely to the least likely. Is there any common agreement? Are there any predictions that are deemed to be highly unlikely or even impossible?

2. Ask the children to work in pairs and to think of other situations that could have several possible outcomes, such as storms, a car accident or shop fire. Tell them to list them. Then ask them to write down the situation and give it to another pair for them to think of the possible outcomes. They have ten minutes to do this. Bring the two pairs back together to discuss their ideas. When they have agreed which is the most likely outcome, ask them to share this with the class. This activity also asks them to think creatively and to use evaluative skills.

Teaching tip

If you can get hold of a crystal ball you could use this as a prop to get the children's attention. Tell them you can predict the future. When they say you can't (because they never believe us, do they!), tell them not only can you, but they can too.

With the first activity you will need to be conscious of the sensitivity of this issue. If you have doubts about talking about it with your children, then replace it with an issue you have dealt with in other PSHE work. It is not the sole intention of this activity to teach the children about the dangers of smoking, though this clearly could be done if you wished, but also to encourage them to look beyond the obvious or preconceived ideas and attitudes they may possess. You should link this skill to the skill of evaluation. That is, that evaluation can be more focused if, at the onset of an activity, one had predicted the possible or intended outcomes.

For the second activity, have ready some suggestions for situations if any groups have not been able to think of any. Encourage them to think of situations that they have experience of, or of situations relevant to work already studied. This will focus their thinking and enable them to reflect upon their own thinking processes in clearer detail. For example, thinking about a situation in which a child has to start in a new class or school does not require the children to make huge leaps in imagination (which is another skill) but to deal with well understood scenarios so they are more likely to be able to remember what they thought, why they thought it and the order of thought (this is metacognition, a vital skill for effective thinkers).

Extension activities

❑ Create activities in which variables may be introduced to provide the opportunity for children to make different predictions. For example:

Divide the class into small groups and tell them they are going to investigate under which conditions bread will keep the freshest. Give each group four pieces of bread. Tell them to put one on a plate and wrap one in clingfilm and to leave these out on the windowsill (or another suitable place in the classroom). Put the third piece on a plate and wrap the fourth piece with clingfilm and put these in a fridge.

Ask the children to predict which piece of bread will go mouldy first, and which will remain the freshest for longest. You may wish to ask them to analyse their results and say which methods of keeping bread fresh are the most effective and draw a conclusion as to why this is.

This extension activity should be a fair test. You may need to give guidance on how to control the variables. Or you could give clear instructions on how to conduct the test so that the actual outcomes are as fair as possible. It is the thinking skills we want the children to focus on as well as the scientific skills needed.

Assessment

• Assess the relevancy of the predictions. Are the children able to list them in order of likelihood?

The ripple effect

Task

Tell the children the following story which contains clues (influencing factors) to the possible consequences of a key action.

> There is a family with two parents and two children. One Friday evening Mum arrives home at the end of her working day. She has brought lots of paperwork home with her that needs doing before Monday.
>
> Dad is a plumber and has parked his plumber's van in the garage.
>
> David, who is seven, has brought the class hamster home to look after it for the weekend.
>
> Joanne, his elder sister who is in her final year at secondary school, is working on her computer writing revision notes for her forthcoming exams.
>
> At the tea table Mum reminds Dad that the freezer is still making a fizzing sound from the plug. He promises he will look at it over the weekend. Dad tells David that he must make sure he feeds the hamster in the morning and clean out the cage. Joanne tells her parents that she is going to a party that night and will be sleeping at her friend's house.
>
> ### Key action/event
>
> During the night when everyone is asleep there is a fire caused by an electrical fault in the freezer, which is kept in the garage.

Ask the children to think about the possible consequences of the fire. They should think about the short-, medium- and long-term consequences of the fire. Ask them to plot the different consequences using this simple ripple effect model.

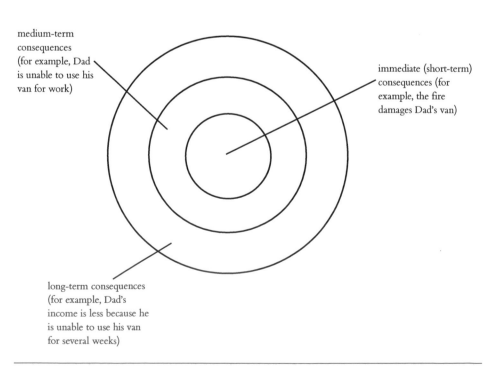

medium-term consequences (for example, Dad is unable to use his van for work)

immediate (short-term) consequences (for example, the fire damages Dad's van)

long-term consequences (for example, Dad's income is less because he is unable to use his van for several weeks)

Teaching tip

Demonstrate the ripple effect by dropping a stone into a bowl of water. Ask the children what they notice happening. Do they notice that as the ripples spread outwards they become weaker but cover a larger area?

It is important to ensure children are familiar both with the vocabulary associated with this activity and the concept of consequence. At the start of the activity suggest simple examples. For example, what might happen if a pool of water is left on the corridor floor? Once the children understand that something can happen as a result of an action, begin to expand on this by demonstrating that there may be another consequence leading from that one. So, using the example above, a child might slip on the wet floor and be hurt. This leads to the child missing a few days of school, which leads to them missing the opportunity to go on a class visit and consequently not being able to do the follow-up activities back at school. The examples you use should be within the likely everyday experiences of the children.

When they are secure in their understanding of consequences and the ripple effect introduce the activity on the facing page. An important element of this activity is the interactive thinking between partners. Ensure your pairings facilitate discussion that is not dominated by one of the pair. After you have read or told them the story, generate a brief class discussion to ensure they have understood what they have to do. Allow about ten minutes for them to discuss the issues between themselves. Then ask them to use the ripple chart to record their thinking. Finish the activity by generating a class discussion.

Extension activities

❑ The children could make up their own stories or situations and a key action or event and either ask others to anticipate possible consequences or do so themselves.

❑ What happens if the key action/event is changed? How do the consequences change?

❑ Look for opportunities in history to explore consequences of major events.

❑ Ask the children to plot out their 'chain' of consequences in cartoon style to develop sequencing skills in literacy and to aid planning stories.

Assessment

- Assess whether the children have been able to identify the immediate consequences of the fire and the subsequent consequences of each of these. For instance, Mum not being able to do her paperwork which might mean her losing her job or losing a contract.

- Some children may only be able to anticipate the immediate consequences, and not necessarily for all of the characters. Some children may focus on the long-term consequences.

- The most able thinkers will be able to identify the immediate consequences and plot the medium-term consequences, which will now result from the new actions and then the long-term consequences.

Enquiry skills:
Testing conclusions

Key skills

- Communication
- Working with others
- Problem solving

Subject links

- Science

Aims

- To enable learners to draw a conclusion and test it.

Organisation

Pairs

Time

30 minutes

Resources

- Sand
- Sandcastle buckets

Outcomes

- The children will have drawn a conclusion as to which mixture creates the best sandcastle and will have tested this using their own idea (or teacher suggestion).

Sandcastles

Task

This activity requires pairs of children to make sandcastles out of two different mixtures of sand and to state which mixture makes the best sandcastle. This in itself is not difficult but the key part of the activity is to test their conclusion as fairly as possible.

Prepare a dry mix of sand, and a damp mix of sand. Ask each pair to make one sandcastle from each mix (some children may need assistance at this stage, and to be reassured if they are unsuccessful, particularly when using the dry mix). Then ask them which mix makes the best castle.

Now tell them that they have drawn a conclusion from what they have done and seen so far. Ask them if they are absolutely sure they are correct. Suggest that they might like to test their conclusion just in case they have experienced a 'fluke' while they made their castles. Ask them to say how they could test their conclusion. Provide broad suggestions if they are unsure how to create a test. Reiterate the importance of a fair test.

Now explain they are going to test their conclusions by making five castles out of each mix and testing them to verify their earlier assertions.

Ask them if they have reached the same conclusion or had to change it.

Bring the pairs together and discuss with them what their conclusions were, how they tested them and the outcome of that testing. Does everyone agree?

Teaching tip

This activity is best carried out under supervision to avoid unnecessary mess or distractions from the set task. You will need to prepare a sufficient amount of the two mixtures of sand for all the pairs to allow a fair test for everyone. The adult supervising the task needs to have the skill to allow the children to experiment with the materials and to discuss their findings and conclusions. The children may need to be prompted to remember the purpose of the task if they are being too distracted by playing with the sand.

It is important that there is the opportunity for all the pairs to discuss their conclusions and to explain how they verified them (explaining how they tested their conclusion), in order to see if there is common agreement across the class.

Ask the children if they can provide examples of when they draw conclusions in real life, and if they ever test them to ensure they have reached the correct conclusion. A simple example would be when a child is presented with a new food and they immediately say they don't like it before they have tasted it.

Extension activities

❑ Read the story of the 'Three Little Pigs' and ask the children to draw a conclusion about the best building materials. Now ask them to design a test to see if their conclusions are correct.

Some children will need assistance at this point. One suggestion is to allow them to build several model houses, each of which is made from an appropriate material as described in the story: straw (or drinking straws), wood (lollipop sticks) and bricks (children's building bricks).

The children then test their constructions and state if their original conclusion was correct.

Assessment

- There are two things to assess. Firstly, if the learner has drawn a conclusion as to which mixture produces the best sandcastle. Secondly, if the learner has tested their conclusion in a fair manner, and if the learner is able to state whether their conclusion was proved to be correct or incorrect in the light of the test carried out.

- More able learners should be able to amend their conclusion in the light of conflicting evidence provided by the test they carried out.

**Enquiry skills:
Testing conclusions**

Key skills

- Communication
- Improving own learning

Subject links

- Science
- Geography
- Maths

Aims

- To understand what a conclusion is.
- To understand that to test and verify conclusions repeated trials must be made.
- To test a range of conclusions and state whether they are valid or not.

Organisation

Whole class and pairs

Time

45 minutes

Resources

- Measuring apparatus
- Maths paper

Outcomes

- The children will have tested a conclusion and judged whether it was valid or invalid.
- The children will know how to test conclusions.

Testing conclusions

Task

Ask the class what the weather is like today. Then say that we could conclude then that 'Every Tuesday is going to be wet' (or whatever the weather is today). Now ask them if that is a reasonable conclusion.

Explain that for a conclusion to be valid it must be tested in repeated trials to see if the same results occur. Now ask them how they could test the conclusion they made about the weather.

Once they have got the idea ask them for other suggestions about conclusions that could be tested, and how they could be tested. For example, all people with blonde hair have blue eyes.

Tell them that a teacher you know came to the following conclusion – that in her class all the children born between September and February are taller than those born between March and August. Now ask the class if they think this is true in all classes. Then ask them how they could test this.

Divide the class into pairs and ask them to carry out a test that will verify or disprove this conclusion.

Tell each pair that they will have to report back to the class explaining their test and the conclusions they have drawn from it. They will also have to provide relevant data to support their conclusion.

Teaching tip

Ensure that the children know what a conclusion is.

Link this skill to the scientific skills of science AT1.

Link this thinking skill with skills in processing information. The conclusion the children draw will be a result of their processing a range of data and information.

This is an ideal opportunity for children to use their ICT skills. They could use them to produce graphs and charts to display the data they collect.

Extension activities

The skill of testing conclusions is closely linked to science, so whenever children are carrying out an AT1 investigation in their science lessons ensure you refer to this skill.

❑ Suggest that girls have better reflexes than boys. Ask for suggestions on how this could be tested. One way is to work in pairs with one child holding their hand out with their first finger and thumb about 7cm to 10cm apart; the second child holds a ruler between the first child's thumb and finger so that the bottom of the ruler is level with the thumb. The second child lets go of the ruler without any warning and the first child has to try and grasp it between their thumb and finger before it falls right through onto the floor. If the first child holds on to the ruler as it falls, the pair makes a note of the place on the ruler where the thumb is holding it. Repeat this exercise five times for each child. Collect the data from the class and ask them to analyse it and state whether the test results validate the original conclusion that girls have better reflexes than boys.

Assessment

- You will need to assess whether the conclusion has been tested thoroughly and if a judgement has been made based upon the evidence provided by the test results. Assess using observation and discussion as the testing is carried out.

Making it better

Task

Tell the children that they are going to improve upon an idea by using their observation and research skills. Ask them to draw a family house and to label the parts.

Then either give them a series of photographs of houses to look at closely, or take them on a walk around your local area to look closely at the houses.

Tell them to look closely at the different parts:

❑ window shapes and sizes
❑ door shapes and sizes
❑ brick patterns
❑ roof shapes
❑ tile patterns

Once they have made notes or sketches of features they have observed, tell them to draw their house again incorporating what they have learned. Talk about how their original ideas have improved.

Teaching tip

Emphasise to the children that it is often possible to improve their original ideas if they use their observational and research skills.

Encourage the children to compare and contrast their original drawings with what they discover through direct observation of a range of houses.

The children can record their ideas and identify the improvements to their original ideas.

Extension activities

❑ You could extend this task by asking the children to draw houses for different purposes. For example:

- a house for a large family
- a house for a family with two cars
- a house for someone who can't climb stairs

Or you could ask them to draw different sorts of buildings. For example:

- shops
- flats
- farms
- schools

Assessment

- Assess if the children have demonstrated improved ideas and if they have identified how their ideas have improved.

**Enquiry skills:
Improving ideas**

Key skills

- Communication
- ICT

Subject links

- Design and technology

Aims

- To use research skills and observation to improve original ideas.

Organisation

Individuals

Time

Three 45 minute sessions

Resources

- Playground brochures and ICT equipment
- Reference materials

Outcomes

- The children will have used research and observation skills to improve original ideas and to produce a final design of a playground/play area.

Playgrounds

Task

Tell the children they are going to design a play area for either the school or the local park. They should draw and label it.

Now tell them that they could probably improve their original idea by conducting some research into how playgrounds are designed and constructed.

Tell them to research the materials used in construction, safety features, joining techniques, sizes, flooring materials, colours and overall appearance, purpose of different apparatus and so on.

Once they have conducted their research and made notes/sketches about what they have found out ask them to draw their design again and incorporate what they have discovered. Also ask them to identify the improvements and label them.

Ask the children to present their designs to the class and to talk about the way they have improved their original designs.

Teaching tip

The essential part of this activity is to ensure that the children have access to sufficient research materials. Schools are regularly sent brochures by companies who design and install playground equipment. Ask your headteacher or school secretary to save them for you. You may also be able to locate these companies on the Internet and browse their sites or request brochures from them. Look in your school and local library as well for books about design. Your local council should also be able to give you information about safety regulations. You could ask the children where they think they might find relevant sources of information. Ideally you should also arrange a visit to a local play area so that the children can observe first-hand well (or in some cases poorly) designed equipment.

Extension activities

This skill can be applied in many different contexts from writing a story to producing a dance sequence in PE. Emphasise the thinking skill as well as the subject skills.

❑ Once the playground designs have been produced, the class could vote on the one they like the best, or you could get the children to build detailed models of them and make a display.

❑ There are several software design packages available for the children to produce their designs on a computer.

Assessment

• Assess whether the children have improved their original ideas and have identified the improvements. You are not assessing the quality of the design but the thinking process that went into the design.

That's a good idea!

Task

Explain to the class that they are going to randomly select some items from a series of boxes and use them to make a model. Ensure they understand that the model can be of anything but that they shouldn't decide what they are going to make before they have all the objects.

Each group then has their 'lucky dips' and then thinks about what they could make using those objects. They record what they intend to make.

They then make their model. Ensure that there are sufficient generic resources, such as string, glue and paper-clips for all the groups. As they are making their models, discuss with them what they are going to make and what made them choose it. If they have changed or extended their original idea, ask them to explain why they have done so.

When they have finished, each group should show the class what they have made and explain how their ideas developed as they made their models.

Teaching tip

You will need to collect a wide range of 'found' objects before this activity can be done. For instance, cereal boxes, plastic bottles, cardboard tubes and straws. Organise the resources into separate boxes so that the children can select one or two items from each box at random. You may want to cover the boxes so that it becomes a 'lucky dip'.

When assessing the final product be aware that it may not be the original intended article. As the activity progressed the children may have had new ideas and made decisions based on the progress they were making at the time. This is an acceptable process and will demonstrate that they have been thinking carefully about their idea and extending it or generating new ones.

Extension activities

❑ Give each pair an object and ask them to think about how it could be changed or improved. For example, a carrier bag could be improved by having stronger handles.

❑ Give each pair an object, such as a teaspoon or a paper-clip, and ask them to think of as many different uses for it as they can.

❑ Show the children a familiar item of clothing, such as a thin coat with no hood. Ask them to work in groups to come up with different ideas for improving the coat for specific purposes. For example, one group could consider how the coat could be improved to make it waterproof. Another group could consider how it could be made to keep out the cold.

Assessment

• Assess if the children are able to describe the finished product and why they chose to create it rather than something else, for example a crocodile rather than a giraffe.

Creative thinking
skills: Generating and
extending ideas

Key skills

- Communication
- Improving own learning and performance
- Problem solving

Subject links

- All subjects have the potential for developing creative thinking.

Aim

- To generate or extend ideas using a random input.

Organisation

Pairs

Time

10 minutes

Resources

- The 'Thinking focus' thinking frame (page 139).
- A pack of random word cards

Outcomes

- The children will have freely created new possibilities from given components.
- The children will be able to demonstrate increased confidence and be able to generate new ideas.

Rubbery ideas!

Task

Decide on the thinking focus for this activity. Ideas might include:

- ❑ different ways to make water go uphill
- ❑ ways to bring about happiness
- ❑ improving the design of a mug
- ❑ reducing litter
- ❑ different ways to catch shop-lifters
- ❑ ways to increase equal opportunities in school
- ❑ improving chairs

Next select a word card from the face down pack as the random input.

So, for the purpose of this demonstration you have chosen 'improving chairs' and the word card 'telescope'.

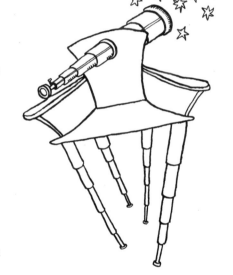

Challenge each pair to create as many new ideas as they can in six minutes. The new ideas may be something like this:

- ❑ chairs with different sections that pull out
- ❑ tubes used as seats
- ❑ chairs attached to the roof so the sitter can watch the stars

The children should record their ideas on the thinking frame on page 139.

Now repeat this using the same thinking focus but with a different random word card.

In the plenary session, discuss with the class the process of thinking undertaken by each pair. Did all the ideas come together in a rush? Did one person's idea spark off another idea? What was happening during the silent moments? Did one idea develop from another?

Teaching tip

The pack of random word cards will need to be changed regularly. The children could suggest words at the beginning of each week, or pick words from a dictionary at random. Nouns, adjectives, adverbs and verbs are best. Don't make qualitative judgements about the children's ideas. This is an open-ended task. Try to create a culture where children can express original ideas with confidence.

Ensure that the thinking time given to the children is short and focused.

Encourage humour within reasonable bounds which should also generate enthusiasm and motivation. Who said learning and thinking can't be fun! Develop appropriate vocabulary to respond to ideas. For example, 'Wow, what a great idea!', 'What an original idea', 'That's an interesting perspective', 'I hadn't thought of it like that' and 'That's really creative.'

Extension activities

❑ Let the children think of their own thinking focus.

❑ Use a current topical news issue as a thinking focus or stimulus.

❑ Take one new idea from the outcome of the task and develop that thought by prioritising it in relation to each of these:

> practicability
> originality
> excitement
> bizarrerie

Then extend the creative idea further. The children could then give a presentation to the class on one selected creative idea. They could describe the processes used, their emotional response to the task and processes and the final outcome.

Assessment

- Observe the number of creative responses and the level of confidence and enjoyment of the children.

**Creative thinking
skills: Hypothesising**

Key skills

- Improving own learning and performance
- Communication

Subject links

- All subjects – reinforcing creativity in all areas of the curriculum

Aims

- To encourage children to pose the question 'I wonder why?' and form a tentative explanation (hypothesis) in answer to the question.

Organisation

Pairs

Time

10–15 minutes

Resources

- None

Outcome

- Children will be able to give a tentative explanation to the question 'I wonder why?'

I wonder why?

Task

Organise the children into pairs. Tell them they are going to work together to pose the question 'I wonder why?' Give them some examples:

- ❑ 'I wonder why we have school uniform?'
- ❑ 'I wonder why cars are different colours?'
- ❑ 'I wonder why polar bears are white?'

The pairs should consider the question and think of an explanation. If each pair thinks of more than one explanation, ask them to decide which is the most likely explanation and which is the least likely.

When everyone is ready, lead a discussion around the various responses given. Value all suggestions but if necessary ask for clarification by asking why they thought of their particular idea. In this way it is possible to assess how children are using prior knowledge and creative ideas.

If the children display a disposition towards further exploration of the issue, in other words they want to test their hypothesis, ask them to think how they might begin to find out if their hypothesis is correct. This should only be done when they have acquired suitable enquiry skills.

When everyone is ready, lead a discussion around the various responses given.

Teaching tip

A dictionary definition of 'hypothesis' is 'A theory that can lead to further enquiry' and 'A tentative explanation of a phenomenon'. Encourage the children to understand that their explanations are only tentative and would need further investigation to establish if their hypotheses are indeed correct. This should encourage self-confidence and a culture in which it is acceptable to voice explanations and be creative in one's thinking. It is the thinking process that you should focus on rather than the accuracy of the explanations. Encourage the children to pose the question as often as possible.

This is a short focused activity so the thinking time given to each pair should be short, about 5–7 minutes.

Extension activities

❑ As the purpose of this activity is to encourage the children to pose the question 'I wonder why?' as a regular and natural element of their creative thinking, why not introduce a 15-minute weekly spot when children themselves pose the question? This allows them to consider issues directly pertinent to their circumstances or interests.

❑ Alternatively, at the end of a lesson ask the children if they have an 'I wonder why?' question about the work they have done or the content of the lesson. Ask the class if they can suggest some explanations to the chosen question. For example, after a PE lesson one child might ask, 'I wonder why when I stand on one leg it is easier if I hold my arms out?'

❑ This question can be particularly effective in PSHE lessons when discussing people's behaviour or attitudes. For example, 'I wonder why some people are bullies?' and 'I wonder why some people smoke?' However, do not allow the questions to be related to a specific named person.

Assessment

• Assess whether children give a hypothesis. The focus is not on the reasonableness of the hypothesis but on the ability to think in a way that leads to one, in other words the thinking process itself. Assessment will be through discussion and careful questioning by the teacher encouraging the children to explain their thinking processes.

The 'Why?' game

Task

Pose a question to the children relating to the local environment. For example:

- ❑ 'Why are the shops situated where they are?'
- ❑ 'Why has our town grown so large?'
- ❑ 'Why are so many lorries passing through our town?'
- ❑ 'Why do people come and visit our town?'

Organise the children into groups and ask them to spend a few minutes discussing the question and arriving at a tentative explanation. They should then record this.

Next they should use the resources provided about the local area to arrive at their final tentative answer.

Then they prepare a short presentation to the class in which they give their answer and explain how they arrived at it.

Finally, each group gives their presentation allowing a short time for others to ask questions about the answer and in particular about the thinking processes used by the group making the presentation.

Let the children challenge the thinking, but only in a sensitive manner. They are not making value judgements about the thinking outcome (hypothesis) but about the thinking processes employed. This will encourage metacognition. For example, 'What made you think of that idea?', 'Did you consider... before you arrived at your explanation?' and 'Did our work in science help you in your thinking?'

Teaching tip

A dictionary definition of 'hypothesis' is 'A theory that can lead to further enquiry' and 'A tentative explanation of a phenomenon.' Encourage the children to understand that at this stage their explanation is only tentative and would need further investigation to establish if their hypothesis is indeed correct. Encourage the habit of questioning 'I wonder why?' The emphasis in this activity is on why children think the way they do rather than on the accuracy of their answers. You will need to tease out of them their reasons for their thinking.

Encourage the children to think about the relevance of knowledge already learned. Give them prompts about work already covered. For example, 'Think about what we learned about coal mining', 'What do you already know about our town?' and 'In what ways can our work on tourism help you arrive at an explanation?'

Extension activities

❑ On Monday mornings hold an 'I wonder why?' session with the whole class. Pose a variety of questions. These can be open-ended with several possible explanations. For example:

'I wonder why it took me 10 minutes longer to get into work today?'

Or they could be questions with specific answers. For example:

'I wonder why rattlesnakes rattle?'

❑ Sometimes you might want to encourage further creative thinking by telling the children that there is a correct answer to the type of question above but you want them to come up with as many ideas of their own (and they can be humorous!) as they can.

❑ The class then has the week to arrive at their answers. At the end of the week the children have the opportunity to give their hypotheses to the class.

Assessment

• Using the short presentation given by each group, assess whether a tentative explanation has been given and if they are able to explain how they arrived at it.

Creative thinking skills: Applying imagination

Key skills

- Communication

Subject links

- English
- Drama

Aims

- To create a story based around three soft toys using imagination.

Organisation

Groups of three

Time

30 minutes

Resources

- Soft toys

Outcomes

- The children will be able to act out their story in role as one of the soft toy characters.

Toy plays

Task

Divide the class into groups of three and give each group three soft toys. Tell them they are going to create a story using these three characters. Say that in this story something important happens to one of the soft toys at home. For example:

❑ They run out of food.
❑ One of the characters has an accident.
❑ There is no heating in the home.

Let the children make their own suggestions as to what the important thing is that happens but if they are unable to think of their own idea give them the examples above and then ask them to think again to find their own idea. Tell them that each of them is going to play the part of one of the soft toys. They must agree who is going to play each of the characters.

Give the children creative thinking time to discuss the plot of their story, what the characters are going to be like and the setting of the story.

Now tell them that they are going to turn their story into a short play for the class.

Give the children time to act out and refine their play in role as the characters.

Then all the groups perform their plays for the class.

Teaching tip

Select soft toy characters that the children can empathise with or are familiar with. If they are not able to think of an important event that could have happened to one of their characters have some ideas already written down on card. The group can then pick one at random and use this as the catalyst for their creative thinking.

In the extension activity encourage the children to use characters that they are familiar with from their reading or literacy lessons.

Extension activities

❑ Give each group three well-known story books and ask each child to pick a one character from each book. Now ask them to create a story using these characters. For example, they could choose Cinderella, the Big Friendly Giant and Flat Stanley. Use the same procedure as for the main activity, ensuring there is an agreed catalyst for their creative thinking.

❑ When doing the main activity, instead of each group deciding the setting for their story, ask another group to provide a setting for the group to use. This should move the thinking away from the familiar towards the unfamiliar and encourage the development of new imaginative ideas.

❑ In pairs ask the children to select a character from a well-known book or story. Then ask them to think about the usual setting for that character. They draw or paint a picture of that character in the familiar setting. Next ask them to think of a setting that would be very unfamiliar to the character, such as the Three Little Pigs now living in a tower block of flats. Ask them to draw or paint a picture of the character(s) in this unfamiliar setting. When these are finished give the pictures to another pair and ask them to create an oral story about the character(s) in this new and unfamiliar setting.

Assessment

- Assess to what degree imagination has been applied. Is the story a mere retelling of a known story or does it show original ideas?

- Assess to what degree imaginative language is used.

Creative thinking
skills: Applying
imagination

Key skills

- Communication
- Problem solving
- Improving own learning and performance
- ICT

Subject links

- Science
- English
- ICT
- Art

Aims

- To create a story that illustrates a scientific concept.

Organisation

Individual

Time

1 hour

Resources

- Word processor
- Drawing software

Outcomes

- The children will have created a fictional piece of writing that illustrates a scientific concept.

Concept stories

Task

Select a scientific concept to be illustrated and tell the class what it is. It could be a subject such as 'evaporation', 'the reflection of light', 'the movement of sound waves' or 'forces'.

Explain to the class that they are going to create a story which must contain references to the concept. This can be through the characters' actions, the dialogue or events in the story. Explain that the purpose is to show the reader that they understand the concept and the manifestations of that concept in real life.

For example, a character who only puts his washing on the line when the weather is wet or very cloudy and cold clearly does not understand about evaporation. However, another character who does understand the concept of evaporation could in some way teach the first how to dry his clothes more efficiently. Alternatively, a shipwrecked character realises that the only way to signal to a passing ship is to reflect the sunlight off a mirrored surface. He hasn't got a mirror so he improvises by using the bottom of a broken glass bottle he finds washed up on the shore.

Allow 15 minutes thinking and planning time and then 45 minutes for the children to write their story.

Once completed let the children read each other's work and act as the critical friend to discuss the levels of imagination applied. They could consider if the concept is clear from the story, and how imaginative the writer has been in illustrating it.

Teaching tip

Use fables as examples of the way an idea/concept can be illustrated. It is done through the writer's imaginative application of the idea. The idea/concept is not explicitly named but apparent through the actions and dialogue of the characters. Once the children are familiar with this they will be more confident in applying their own imagination to illustrate concepts.

Younger Key Stage 2 children can do this activity in pairs, and orally recount their story.

In the extension drawing task emphasise to the children that they are not producing a diagram with labels but a 'concept picture'.

Extension activities

❑ Instead of writing a story the children draw a 'concept picture' to illustrate the scientific concept.

❑ Challenge the children to design a logo for the concept. Provide them with well-known examples of logos to discuss.

❑ Set the class a 10-minute challenge to think of as many alternative uses as they can for a paper-clip. Or you can use any common household object.

❑ Tell the class that they each have to think of one superhuman power they would like, such as being invisible, super strong or super fast. They have to think of as many ways as they can of how they could use this power for the benefit of others. And the ways this power could be used to the detriment of others.

Assessment

- Assess whether the scientific concept is clear to the reader.
- Assess the degree of imagination that has been applied.
- It is also possible to use this activity to assess the level of understanding of the scientific concept itself.

Key skills

- Communication

Subject links

- Science
- Literature

Aims

- To select and use a range of animal features to produce an original creature that incorporates these features.

Organisation

Individual

Time

30 minutes

Resources

- Photos of a wide range of animals

Outcomes

- The children will have drawn a picture of a hybrid animal they have created.

New animals

Task

Explain to the class that they will each be given three pictures of animals and that they are to select one feature from each animal. The purpose is to create a new creature that utilises each of these features in some way to assist it in its life. For example, if they have pictures of an elephant, a cat and a butterfly they might select the trunk from the elephant, claws from the cat and wings from the butterfly. They then have to combine these features and create a new animal that incorporates these features.

The new animal could then use its wings to reach the tops of taller trees, where it wants to suck out the grubs from the holes in the tree trunk using its trunk.

The children then have to draw their newly created creature in as much detail as possible.

Each child then shows their creature to the class and explains why each feature was chosen and how it assists the new creature. Also ask the children to give a name to their creature. Let the class ask questions and act as critical friends.

Teaching tip

Encourage and provide positive reinforcement for original ideas expressed.

Don't evaluate on a qualitative judgement of the outcome, ie the quality of the drawing, the accuracy of the proportions of each feature or the anatomical placement of the key features (the trunk could be on the back of the new creature instead of the front of the head). Instead try to identify the thinking processes employed. Ask the children to explain why they chose each feature. What was the purpose of the feature in the original animal and what will it be in the new creature? Has the new creature used it for a different purpose? Why is it in a different position on the new animal?

Extension activities

❏ Ask the children to write or tell alternative endings to fairytales or stories.

❏ Ask the children to retell a story they have read or know. Then give the class a key influencing factor to be introduced into the story. Ask them how the story might have ended differently if this new key factor had been introduced. For example, a terrible storm raged during the period of the story or one of the main characters fell ill in the middle of the story. Give the class these factors until they are confident enough to suggest their own. Ask for possible alternative endings or outcomes.

Assessment

- Assess if the children have identified one feature from each of the three given animals and if these are clear in the new hybrid creature they have created.

- Assess how innovative the outcome is.

What would happen if...?

Creative thinking skills: Looking for alternative outcomes

Key skills

- Communication
- Working with others

Subject links

- Science
- History

Aims

- To select and use knowledge to create an original outcome.

Organisation

Individual

Time

45 minutes

Resources

- Photos or examples of a wide range of plants

Outcomes

- The children will have drawn a detailed illustration with labels of a hybrid plant they have created.

Task

Introduce the activity by asking the class to consider why flowers are brightly coloured. This feature serves a valuable purpose for the flower – to attract insects so that pollination can occur. Can the children think of alternative purposes for this feature? Encourage them to be as imaginative as they can. For instance, some flowers are brightly coloured so that short-sighted people walking through the garden won't tread on them and kill them.

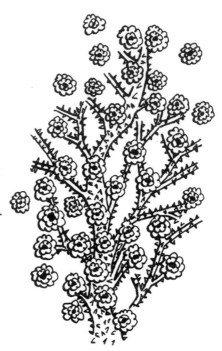

Ask the class to think of another plant, a cactus, and ask them what features it may have and what purposes these features serve. Again encourage imaginative alternative functions for these features.

Once the children understand what features are and that they always serve a purpose for the plant, give each child three pictures of different plants. Ask them to select one feature from each of the three plants. For example, one child selects thorns from a rose, cup shaped leaves from a pitcher-plant and helicopter shaped seeds from a sycamore tree.

Tell them that they now have to combine these features to create a new plant. This new plant will also have some features common to all or most plants, such as leaves, stems and roots. They should also think of a name for this new plant.

The children should draw their newly created plant and label it carefully. The labels should indicate the three original features and the way the new plant uses them. Are they now used for a different imaginative purpose?

Each child exhibits their drawing and gives a short presentation to the class. Allow for questions from the class. Encourage the children to explain why they chose each feature and its role in the hybrid plant. If they have created a new purpose for the feature can they explain their thinking? Why will it be useful to the new plant? How did they come to imagine a new function for the feature? For instance, thorns may have been used as a form of defence by the original plant but as the thorns look like arrow-heads the plant could fire these as a form of attack, like using a bow and arrow.

Teaching tip

Encourage with positive reinforcement for original ideas.

Don't evaluate on a qualitative judgement of the outcome, ie the quality of the drawing or the accuracy of the proportions of each feature. Instead try to identify the thinking processes employed. Ask the children to explain why they chose each feature. What was the purpose of the feature in the original plant and what will it be in the new plant? Has the new plant used it for a different purpose? Why is it in a different position on the new plant? Has the child only used the feature for its original purpose or have they actively thought about alternative uses?

Extension activities

❏ Challenge children to think about what Britain might be like today if Germany had won the Second World War.

❏ Or what might happen if petrol cost £20 a litre.

❏ Challenge the children to devise their own 'What might happen?' questions for the class to think about.

Assessment

- Assess whether the selected features from the original plants can be identified.

- Is the illustration labelled accurately and informatively?

- How innovative is the newly created outcome?

Evaluation skills: Evaluating information

Key skills

- Communication
- Improving own learning and performance

Subject links

- All subjects in which information has to be processed, in order to answer a question
- Geography

Aims

- To enable the learner to make an evaluation as to whether the information processed has been useful in answering a question.

Organisation

Pairs or small groups

Time

30 minutes

Resources

- Information sources on farms (or your own chosen topic)

Outcomes

- The children will be able to state whether the information used has enabled them to answer a question.

How good is my information?

Task

Ask the children to write down (or tell you) three questions about farms (or any other topic chosen by you) that they would like to know the answers to. For example:

❑ At what time of year are lambs born?
❑ How much milk does a cow produce?
❑ How are straw bales made?

Now provide them with some sources of information that will help them to find the answers to their questions. (Alternatively, ask them to locate possible useful sources.)

After allowing them time to examine the information sources ask them to record (or tell you) their answers.

Discuss with them how useful the information was.

❑ Did it help them to answer the questions?
❑ How did it help?
❑ Was the information easy to find?
❑ Was the information easy to understand?
❑ Was it the text or the pictures that helped?
❑ Do they need more information before they can answer the questions?
❑ What would they do next if the information did not help them answer the questions?

Teaching tip

This is the first stage of a complex skill and the children will need lots of opportunities to become aware of the importance of evaluating their work/learning. If, at the beginning of the lesson, you share with them the learning objective, at the end of the lesson you can help them to evaluate whether they have achieved the objective. This will establish the regular practice of evaluation.

This activity makes the connection between the process of answering a question and the actual outcome. In order to answer the question the children will need to process some information. The children are encouraged to judge whether the information has been useful in answering the question. If not, then they are asked if they need more information. In Key Stage 1 the children are only required to state 'Yes' or 'No' to the question 'Has the information helped me to answer the question?' In Key Stage 2 the children are required to state how it has been useful.

Extension activities

This is such a crucial part of the learning process that learners should be encouraged to evaluate all information they use. Therefore, the extension activities are in effect all or any of the work the learner does.

❑ The interpretation and understanding of text is an integral part of the Literacy Strategy and the evaluation of text is a logical extension of that.

❑ The children will be required to use information in a range of forms, not just text. In science and maths, numerical data and graphs/charts will be used. There is still a need to evaluate its use in providing answers to questions. More able Key Stage 1 children could be introduced to the idea of evaluating how the information has helped them in terms of what they now know and understand.

❑ You could reverse the process of the activity above by providing the children with some information and asking them to write three questions that could be answered by using it. They can check the validity of their questions by asking another child, or group, to find the answers to the questions using the same information. Then ask them to discuss with each other how useful the information was, or if there are any other questions they could have posed.

Assessment

- The children should record the question, whether the information processed has been useful or not, and their answer. Discuss with them how the information was useful and whether further information is required.

Evaluation skills:
Evaluating
information

Key skills

- Communication
- Improving own learning

Subject links

- Literacy
- All subjects

Aims

- To enable the children to evaluate whether the information processed has been useful in helping them to learn and to answer questions.
- To enable the children to evaluate what the information has helped them understand and know.

Organisation

Pairs/groups

Time

30-40 minutes

Resources

- Television listings from different sources

Outcomes

- The children will have evaluated how useful the information has been in answering questions and helped to develop understanding and knowledge.

How good is my information?

Task

Provide the groups/pairs with a copy of a day's television listings (or two different sources of this information, such as the *Radio Times* and today's newspaper).

Now ask them to answer the following questions (or think of your own questions).

❑ How often is the news on during the day?
❑ Is the film (select one) on at (give time and channel) suitable for children under the age of 11?
❑ How many documentaries (or comedies/dramas) are on today?

After allowing sufficient time ask them to give their answers.

Explain that the important part of this activity is to evaluate the usefulness of the information. Discuss with them:
❑ whether the information provided helped them answer all the questions or some of them
❑ how it helped
❑ why it did not help answer some of the questions
❑ what it has helped them understand
❑ what it has helped them know

Teaching tips

Evaluation should be an expected regular part of the learning process. With younger or less able learners the exercise can be done orally as part of a plenary session.

Initially the children will need to be taught how to evaluate information. Ultimately they should become independent thinkers and use the process in all the work they do.

You will need to ensure that the children are clear about the difference between understanding and knowledge. Knowledge is known facts. Understanding is making connections between facts and being able to apply knowledge to different contexts.

Extension activities

Making judgements about the relative use of information is such a crucial part of the learning process that learners should be encouraged to evaluate all information they use. Therefore, the extension activities are in effect all or any of the work the learner does.

❑ The activity could be extended by asking the groups to set each other questions using the information provided.

❑ The interpretation and understanding of text is an integral part of the Literacy Strategy and the evaluation of text is a logical extension of that.

❑ Learners will be required to use information in a range of forms, not just text. In science and maths, numerical data and graphs/charts will be used. There is still a need to evaluate its use in providing answers to questions and extending understanding and knowledge. Processing the wealth of information on the Internet requires the learner to evaluate quickly whether a particular site, or web page, is going to be useful or not; or to use a site and then make an evaluation in order to recommend it to others as a useful site.

Assessment

• As well as assessing whether the children have been able to answer the questions, you should be assessing if they can identify if the information has helped them answer all or some of the questions. Can they state how it helped or did not help and what it has helped them understand and know?

Evaluation skills: Judging the value of what is heard, seen and done

Key skills

- Communication
- Improving own learning and performance

Subject links

- All subjects

Aims

- To enable the children to evaluate how good their work is, and what they are pleased with.

Organisation

Individual

Time

5-10 minutes per child

Resources

- The children's own work

Outcomes

- The children are able to state what pleases them about a particular piece of work.
- The children are able to state how they could improve their work.

How good is my work?

Task

Tell the children that you are going to show them how they can evaluate the work they have done at school. Ask one child to come to the front of the class with a recent piece of work. Ask the child what they were asked to do and if they were able to do it. Now ask them what they are pleased with, quite pleased with or not happy with.

At this stage they might not be able to give clear reasons for their opinions.

Next ask them to say how they could make their work even better.

Repeat this with another child.

The above can be included in any plenary session, as long as the learning objective has been made explicit to the class at the start of the lesson.

Teaching tip

At this stage you are asking the children to make a value judgement of their work. In Key Stage 2 they will be required to give reasons for their judgements.

Ensure that the process of self-evaluation is treated sensitively. The purpose is both to celebrate achievement and to identify how the learner will be able to move forward in their learning and development of skills.

If you have a system of keeping records of achievement then this activity will enhance the process and emphasise the importance of putting the child at the centre of the learning process.

The concept of evaluating one's own outcomes and work can be introduced as part of plenary sessions as long as objectives are shared with the class at the start of the session. Then the teacher can work with individual learners to help them become confident in self-evaluation, and to help set targets for future work.

Extension activities

❑ To encourage confidence and to emphasise the importance of evaluation, ask the children to discuss their work with others. This could be done either in pairs:

Child A has completed some work. Child B asks Child A what they have achieved and what they are pleased with, quite pleased with and not pleased with. They also discuss with them how they could improve their work. Then Child B reports back to the class by celebrating Child A's work and explaining what was good about it and how Child A will improve it next time. This reinforces the process of target setting and places the learner at the heart of it.

or as part of plenary sessions where groups have been engaged in different or similar tasks:

Each group discusses with another group what they have done, why they are pleased with it and so on. Then the groups report back to the class what they have discovered about each other's work, and whether the learning objective(s) has been met.

Assessment

- At this stage you need to assess if the children are able to examine their work and state what pleases them about it. You may be able (with more able learners) to get them to begin to say why it pleases them. Your assessment for this activity will be through discussion and gentle probing.

How will I know how good my work is?

Evaluation skills: Judging the value of what is heard, seen and done

Key skills

- Communication
- Improving own learning and performance

Subject links

- All subjects

Aims

- To enable the child to evaluate their own work by stating what they are pleased with, and to give reasons for their opinions.
- To enable the child to identify how their work could be improved.

Organisation

Individual

Time

5–10 minutes per child

Resources

- The children's own work
- The thinking frame on page 140

Outcomes

- The children are able to state what pleases them about a particular piece of work and their reasons for their evaluation.
- The children are able to state how they could improve their work.

Task

Tell the children that you are going to show them how they can evaluate the work they have done at school. Ask one child to come to the front of the class with a recent piece of work. Ask them what they were asked to do and if they were able to do it.

Now ask them what they are pleased with, quite pleased with and not happy with.

Encourage them to give reasons for their opinions. Ask them to identify the skills they have used and the knowledge they have learned (relate these to previous objectives set, the current ones and previous targets).

Next ask them to say how they could make their work even better. Help them to turn these ideas into targets for them to achieve and suggest a timescale for completion. They could record their thinking using the frame on page 140.

Repeat this with another child.

The above can be included in any plenary session, as long as the learning objective has been made explicit to the class at the start of the lesson.

Teaching tip

If you have a system of keeping records of achievement then this activity will enhance the process and emphasise the importance of putting the learner at the centre of the learning process.

The concept of evaluating one's own outcomes and work can be introduced as part of plenary sessions as long as objectives are shared with the class at the start of the session. Then the teacher can work with individual children to help them become confident in self-evaluation, and to help set targets for future work.

Extension activities

❑ To encourage confidence and to emphasise the importance of evaluation ask the children to discuss their work with others. This could be done either in pairs:

Child A has completed some work. Child B asks Child A what they have achieved, what they are pleased with, quite pleased with and not pleased with and the reasons for their judgements. They also discuss with them how they could improve their work. Then Child B reports back to the class by celebrating Child A's work and explaining what was good about it and how Child A will improve it next time. This reinforces the process of target setting and places the learner at the heart of it.

or as part of plenary sessions where groups have been engaged in different or similar tasks:

Each group discusses with another group what they have done, why they are pleased with it and so on. Then the groups report back to the class what they have discovered about each other's work, and whether the learning objective(s) has been met.

Assessment

- If the child can state what pleases them about their work, but is not able to give valid reasons for this opinion then they are still working at KS1 level (see the KS1 activity on page 124).

- If they are able to give valid reasons for their judgements, assess the quality of the thinking by referring to the objectives of the lesson and the purpose of the task. Is the child able to highlight some of the key skills they have employed? Does the child identify key knowledge they have acquired?

- Now assess if the child has been able to state how they could improve their work. Are they able to identify weaknesses, and are they able to identify the next step in their development of skills and knowledge? If they are not able to do this, then set the targets with them and remind them to evaluate their future work to judge whether these have been met.

Being a guide

Task

Tell the children to imagine that they have to act as a guide to a new child in the class. The first part of their task is to draw a simple map of the school. The second is to write a simple guide to the school day.

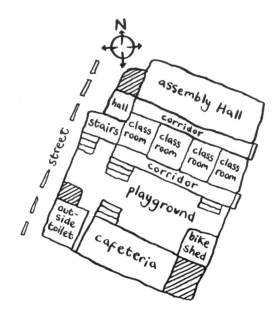

Now discuss with the children the sorts of things they need to do in preparation for the task and what they will include in their map and guide.

Next, discuss with them what 'criteria' are and ask them to suggest what criteria they can identify to judge whether they have completed the task successfully. For example:

❑ The map is labelled or has a key.
❑ The guide includes details of the times lessons start and end, lunch-times, playtimes and so on.
❑ The map can be used to help the new child to find their way from the classroom to the office and back again.
❑ The guide can be understood by poorer readers as well as good readers.

Now allow them to complete their map and guide.

Next ask them to refer back to their criteria and complete the thinking frame.

Teaching tip

The activity will need to take place over more than one lesson. Use the first one to set the criteria and prepare the map/guide. Use the second and third for the children to produce their maps/guides. Use the fourth/final lesson to evaluate how successful they have been by referring back to the criteria for success.

Use the results of your assessments to help the children set targets for future learning. The criteria they do not meet will inform you of these.

Extension activities

❑ Use this format for identifying criteria to judge how successful the children have been in different lessons. Once they are familiar with objectives being set then they can use this skill to focus their own self-evaluation.

Assessment

- Assess whether the child has identified at least two criteria to apply in their evaluation.

- Assess whether the child has identified what criteria have been met/not met.

The planning frame

Name

I did this as part of my work on

Sort tanks

I did this as part of my work on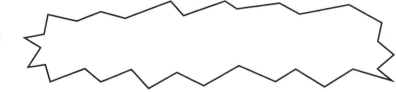

Name it

Name _____

I did this as part of my work on

Name _____   Date _____

Stepping stones

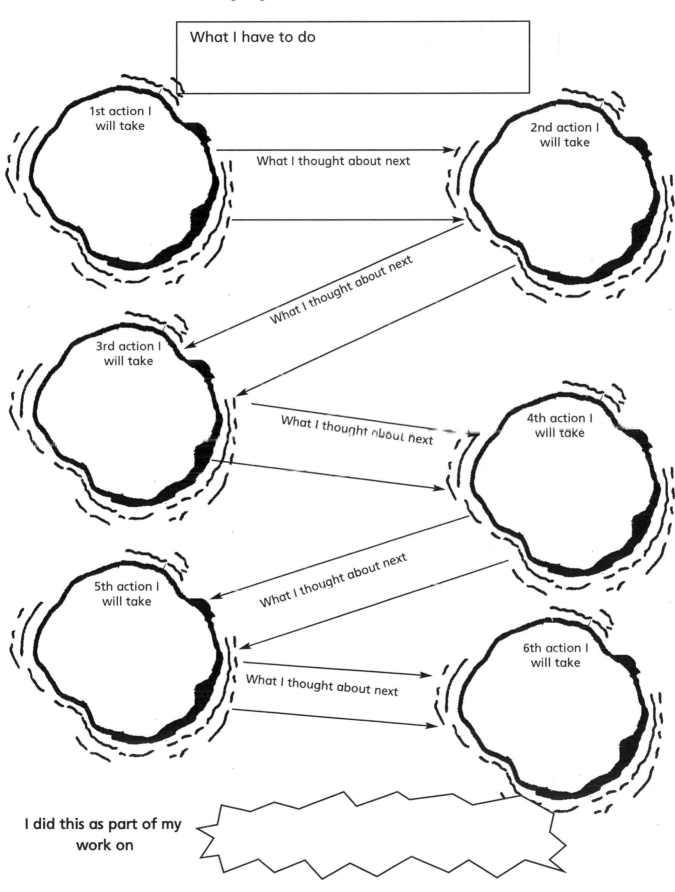

What I have to do

1st action I will take

What I thought about next →

2nd action I will take

What I thought about next

3rd action I will take

What I thought about next

4th action I will take

What I thought about next

5th action I will take

What I thought about next

6th action I will take

I did this as part of my work on

Name _____

Date _____

Links

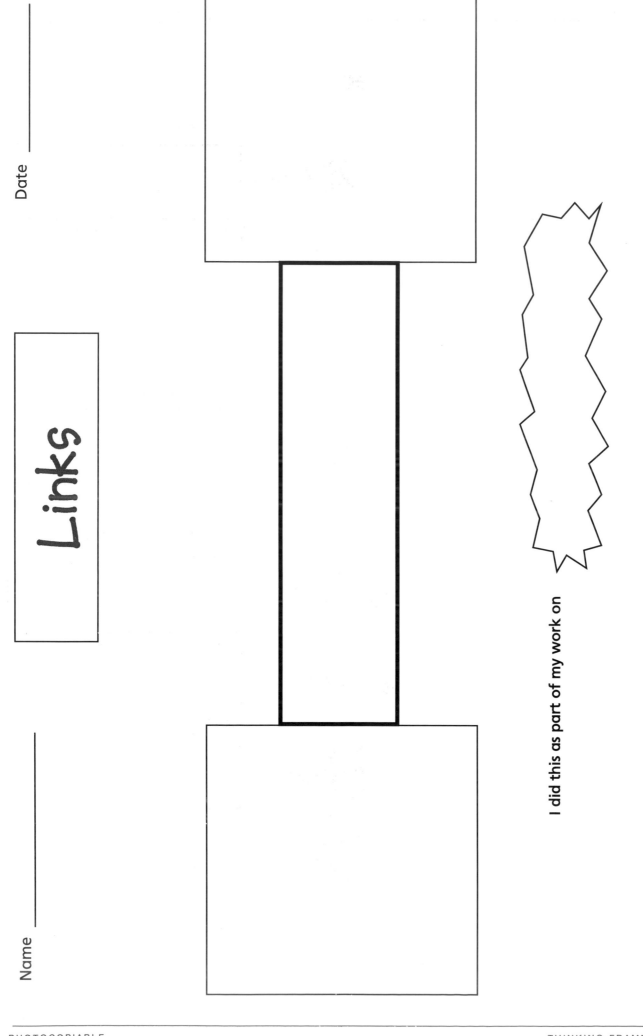

I did this as part of my work on

Name _____   Date _____

Because

I think this   **Reasons for opinions**

	because →	

	because →	

	because →	

	because →	

I did this   **Reasons for actions**

	because →	

	because →	

	because →	

	because →	

I did this as part of my work on

The time capsule

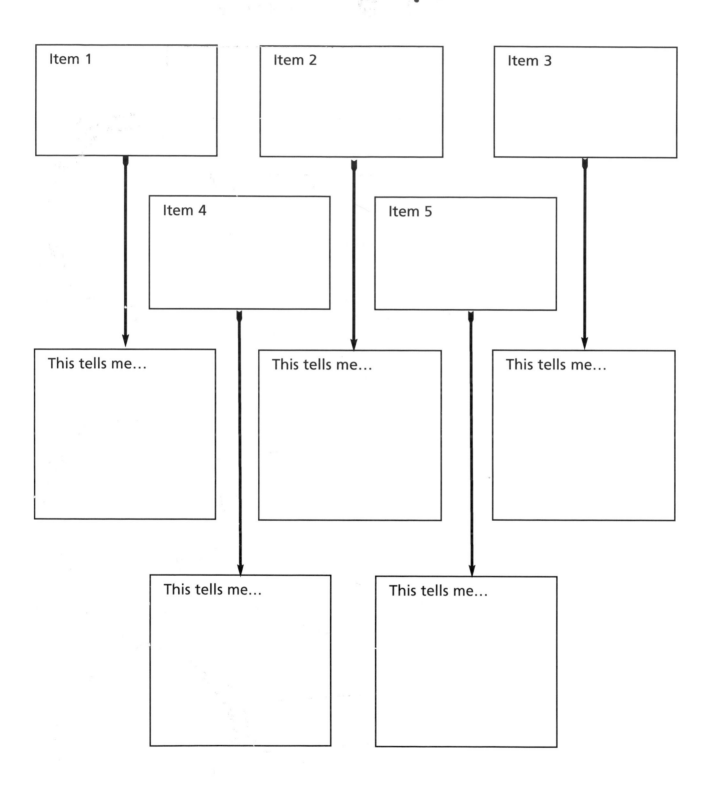

| Item 1 | Item 2 | Item 3 |

| Item 4 | Item 5 |

This tells me…

This tells me…

This tells me…

This tells me…

This tells me…

I think this time capsule belonged to…

Stepping stones - 2

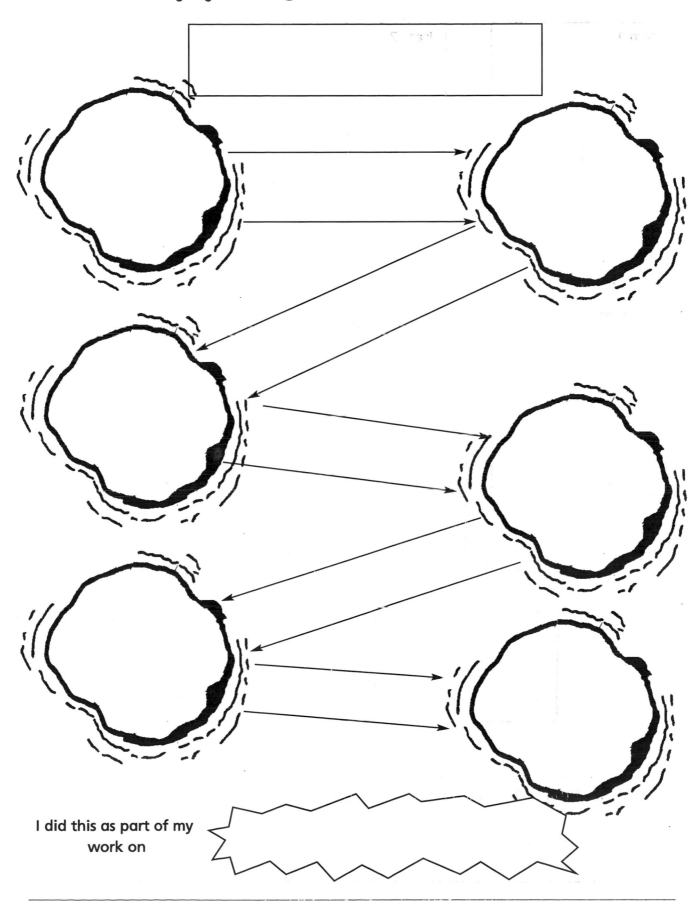

I did this as part of my work on

The ripple effect

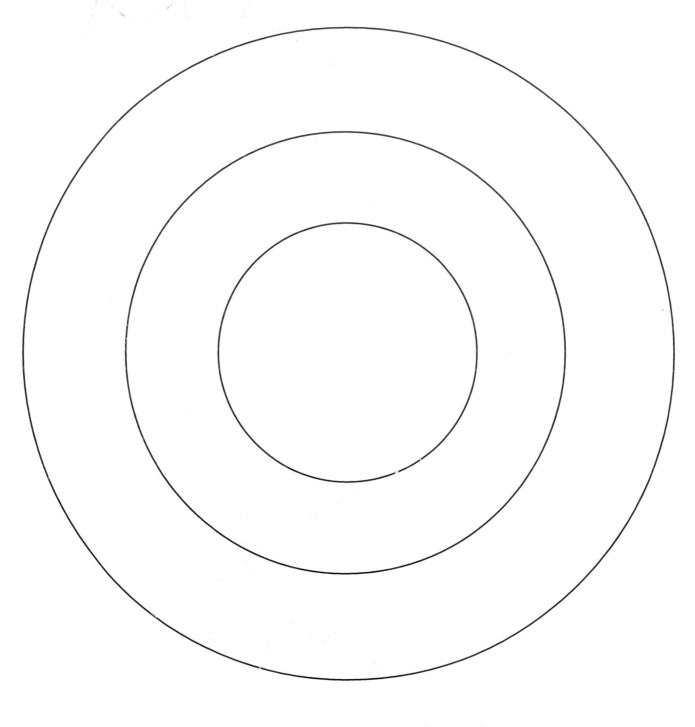

I did this as part of my work on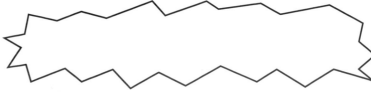

Date _____

Thinking focus

Today I have been thinking about...

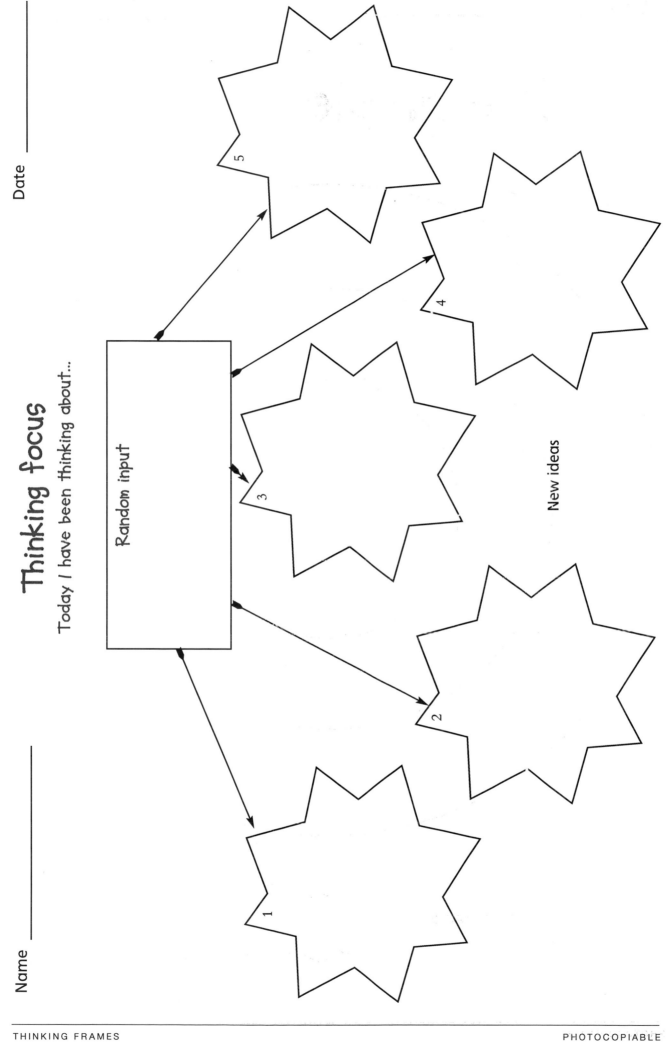

Random input

New ideas

1

2

3

4

5

Name _____

I have looked carefully at this work...

What I'm pleased with

What I'm quite pleased with

What I'm not pleased with

What I will try to do better next time

How I will try to do this